Praise for C
Get Into Cla

'If you like classical mus
more about it, a new
A splendid introduction to enable you
to select your favourite pieces'

Daily Express

'If you need the lowdown on Liszt, the chat on
Tchaikovsky; if you want to be briefed
on Beethoven, primed on Prokofiev,
versed in Vivaldi, this is the
book to read'

What's On

'A nifty little paperback may prove the ideal
gift . . . A non-intimidating introduction
for people who want to know where to
start and what to hear'

Classical Music

'Forget rock, forget rap, pin back your lugholes
and tune into classical music. Grab a copy of
Get Into Classical Music . . . this handy
little book gives you the lowdown and puts a name
to all those familiar tunes you hear
but can't put a name to'

More

'A clever idea well done'

Today

Also by Chris Craker

Get Into Classical Music

Get Into Opera

Chris Craker

BANTAM BOOKS
TORONTO • NEW YORK • LONDON • SYDNEY • AUCKLAND

GET INTO OPERA

Based on an original concept by
Chris Craker and Mark Chapple

A BANTAM BOOK 0 553 40539 X

First publication in Great Britain

PRINTING HISTORY
Bantam Books edition published 1992
Bantam Books edition reprinted 1993

Set in 11/14½pt Monotype Plantin by Kestrel Data, Exeter

Bantam Books are published by Transworld Publishers Ltd.,
61–63 Uxbridge Road, Ealing, London W5 5SA,
in Australia by Transworld Publishers (Australia) Pty. Ltd.,
15–25 Helles Avenue, Moorebank, NSW 2170,
and in New Zealand by Transworld Publishers (N.Z.) Ltd.,
3 William Pickering Drive, Albany, Auckland.

Printed and bound in Great Britain by
Cox & Wyman Ltd., Reading, Berks.

This book is dedicated to my parents

Author's Note
and
Acknowledgements

A few years ago, if you'd asked the average man or woman on the street whether they had ever heard any music by Puccini, it's highly likely the question would have met with a pretty blank expression. Now, in the aftermath of the *Three Tenors* spectacle at Italia '90 and Luciano Pavarotti's unrivalled success with '*Nessun dorma*', millions of people would now even be able to sing you a bit of Puccini.

This book is for those of you who like what you've heard and want to find out a bit more. What else did Puccini write that was as appealing as '*Nessun dorma*'? How to set about unravelling the fast-moving plot of a comic opera such as Mozart's *Marriage of Figaro* when you don't understand a word of Italian. Do you have to spend your life savings on a ticket to the opera to get the best from this music? The answers to these and many other questions are to be found in these pages.

My thanks go once again to Mark Chapple for his unfailing energy and enthusiasm; to Olivia Ma for her assistance and valued advice; to my wife Kate for putting up with the incessant rattle of the computer keys and also to the very helpful staff at English National Opera.

Chris Craker
May 1992

Contents

Introduction

The rise in popularity of classical music shows no sign of waning and in recent years we have seen a remarkable resurgence of interest in the specific medium of opera. Two centuries ago opera was very much the music of the people – only in the last fifty years or so did it come to be regarded by many as an élitist and upper class art-form – and Italian composers such as Rossini, Donizetti and Bellini, with Wolfgang Amadeus Mozart from Austria, held almost cult status as celebrated tunesmiths. Everyone – people from all walks of life – enjoyed and appreciated the work of these and many other talented composers.

Opera performances were genial affairs that provided a welcome opportunity for socializing, eating and drinking as well as the delights of the opera itself. The aristocracy of the day were also very keen on, and particularly supportive of, opera. Often performances would take place in their palaces or stately homes, following their sponsoring, or, indeed, commissioning, of the operas. Here we see one curious parallel with the presentation of opera today: wealthy individuals or business corporations are relied upon to provide the financial backbone for many classical music performances (opera in particular) and, by the very nature of this practice, money is the root of the 'exclusivity problem'.

The price of a ticket to the opera is now well out of the

reach of most people: the main reasons are the increasing degree of sophistication in the productions staged and the expansion of the network around the world of large, purpose built opera houses each requiring numerous administrative staff and each having huge overheads, including 'rate' bills or their equivalent, and advertising costs. Then, of course, there are very substantial payments to the orchestra, chorus and solo artists. When one bears in mind that the top opera stars of today can individually command in excess of £15–20,000 per performance, it is clear that ticket prices do inevitably have to be set high in order to make opera houses viable. In most cases large state subsidies are also needed to help balance the books.

The last couple of years have witnessed a major change in the popularity and profile that opera is achieving. This is largely attributable to the efforts of four highly paid opera stars (together with their respective record companies and marketing advisers) who have reawakened the public's interest in the music from their world. Luciano Pavarotti, Placido Domingo, José Carreras and Kiri Te Kanawa can almost alone take the credit for this revival of enthusiasm through their success in bringing opera directly to the people.

The overwhelming response to the work of these artists has given rise to an enormous amount of media coverage monitoring the rise in popularity of classical music in general and the diverse activities of these four opera stars in particular. Many of these reports have expressed astonishment and disbelief at the phenomenon, but what's the big surprise? This is a form of artistic expression that has stood the test of time for one very good reason: it's great music with which everyone can identify and by which everyone can be emotionally moved, *if given the chance*. There lies the key to this whole issue. We have all had our eyes opened to the world of classical music and opera in a way that is relevant and fitting to society today. Opera tunes and all styles of classical music have been used by the cinema, radio and television, thereby whetting the appetite of people who are uninterested in the pop scene and are seeking alternative music to play on their gleaming new CD and cassette machines. We've returned to a point where most people could hum you a bit of Puccini, but if you've enjoyed listening to a piece and don't know where to turn in your search for more of the same, what do you do next?

The price issue and the unease felt by the average person about going to the Royal Opera House (or where-ever), even if able to afford it, are the two main problems here. In the last year or so, however, various forward-thinking promoters have started staging classical music concerts and operas at venues in which this new mass audience feels at home. The operas are presented as 'spectacular events', which they are – and always have been. I take my hat off to these promoters for opening up this whole world of music that has until now been something of a closed shop for most people.

Apart from attending one of these more affordable 'spectacular events' which will only happen once or twice a year, there are two other steps into the world of opera – namely video (on which all the famous operas are now available) or recordings, although with the latter you obviously miss out on the visual involvement. Let me be clear here: there's nothing quite like experiencing the real thing and I wholeheartedly recommend anyone who has never been to an opera to make every effort to attend a live performance if possible. Nevertheless, the fact that enormous numbers of boxed sets of opera CDs are selling at an ever increasing rate shows there is a growing and very enthusiastic following for this multifaceted art-form and this book is both for people who are planning to go to an opera and those who will listen at home.

To get the most out of experiencing opera, a bit of effort is required. You could of course just sit back, relax and enjoy the music, but I strongly urge you to gain a deeper understanding of the subject. You will further your enjoyment by following the way the plot develops (since most operas you listen to will be in a foreign language) and appreciating how the composer uses musical devices to heighten the dramatic effect. These and many other subjects will be addressed in the coming pages with the aim of making your approach to opera smooth and uncomplicated.

The chief purpose of this book is to assist this process by dispelling some of the myths and mystique surrounding the subject. We will begin with opera from the late eighteenth century (for reasons that will become more apparent later). But before we come to the main business of the book, after this Introduction there follows a chapter which explains the technical terms that feature in all aspects of operas. Some readers may already be familiar with these, but I think it's important for others taking their very first steps not to feel daunted by, or excluded from, the subject simply because they are not *au fait* with the jargon.

We then move on, through the chapter describing the music found on the CD and cassette *Get Into Opera*, and to the main part of the book, *The Composers and Their Operas*. Some historical background on the composers is included and, where it's particularly interesting or relevant, I've taken a closer look at their lives and times. We'll explore, in some detail, the plots and musical construction of the operas from which the *Your Starter Top Ten* are drawn; this way you will see how each composer approached the task of writing the opera and at the same time you will get a taste of most of the highly popular operatic styles from different nationalities. By definition, my selection is made up of my own personal choices but I feel sure these specific examples are ones that will be enjoyed by all. Operas by other mainstream composers, the less well-known works and others are touched upon later, in the chapter *Where Next?*

Since many readers will use this book as a guide to what to listen to on recordings, having been motivated by the likes of the 'Three Tenors', it's worth pointing out that there are numerous recorded versions of highlights from each of the famous operas dealt with here. Purists might scoff at my even condoning such products but I take the standpoint that if you're happier listening to *The Best Of* . . . then why not? It's an undeniable fact that a high percentage of people who enjoyed Pavarotti's recording of '*Nessun dorma*' will not want to listen to the whole opera *Turandot* by Puccini. It would be wonderful if, as a result of reading this book and listening to the featured arias and music on the accompanying CD or tape, your appetite was whetted enough to give it a go, but no-one should feel in the least bit guilty about not becoming an opera buff *per se*. Enjoying the music is the important thing and I hope very much that this book will help you on your way. It's not intended to be the 'definitive guide'; my aim has been to provide an easily digestible overview to give you a taste of what else is on offer if you've enjoyed the bits of opera that you've come across so far.

If, however, you do become more than an armchair viewer or listener and you plan to go to the opera, there are one or two other issues to bear in mind. The first thing to do, having made your choice of opera and venue, is to get your tickets well in advance. Quite often, as with major pop and sporting events, tickets sell out within days or, even, hours of going on sale, so forward planning is essential. It's also advisable to arrive in plenty of time for the performance. The last thing you want is to find yourself hurrying and therefore unable to soak up the atmosphere of the occasion. Most people dress up to go to the established opera houses, but to the recent performances of *Turandot* at Wembley Arena, people turned up in jeans. Times certainly have changed and the main thing is for you to be yourself, feel comfortable and enjoy the spectacle. Another good reason for arriving early is to allow yourself time to buy a copy of the programme. Unless you're totally familiar with the plot of the opera it's wise to read the synopsis so that you'll know exactly what's going on. Later in this book there are down-to-earth accounts of the stories for ten of the most popular operas, so if your first visit to the opera features one of these you'll find you have a head start.

The vast majority of operas are in foreign languages and performances are presented either in their original language (in which case it's imperative to be fully conversant with the plot) or in translated versions. Sometimes those sung in English sound a little odd as, inevitably, translated phraseology doesn't quite fit the music and compromises have to be made. At some opera houses, a video display provides a translation to accompany the lines being sung. Some members of the audience find this a great help, but for others it's an irritating distraction. Whatever your personal preference in this respect, I hope the translations in this book are useful.

Not only have such superlative artists such as Pavarotti, Domingo, Carreras and Kiri Te Kanawa contributed enormously to the process of making opera more accessible to today's new mass audience, they have also played a large part in such enterprises as free concerts, cross-over projects linked to popular shows and, more recently, performances of non-operatic music with words added. Whatever the purists may say about such activities, no-one can deny that these four artists have changed the public's perception of classical music and in so doing, they have paved the way for us all to *Get Into Opera*.

Get Into Opera

CHAPTER ONE

What Exactly Is Opera?

The Concise Oxford Dictionary of Music defines opera as 'a drama set to music – entirely or partially, but in either case in such a degree that the musical part of the entertainment ranks as an essential, and not an incidental, element.'

The word opera is derived from the Latin opus meaning 'work'. We can think of an opera as a 'work of art' – a unique blend of theatrical play and vivid visual drama set to music. In this book we deal mostly with operas dating from the late eighteenth century but remember that the earliest derivatives of the medium go as far back as the twelfth century, culminating in what we commonly perceive as opera in about 1600. The first works were written by the Italian composers Corsi, Peri and Caccini, but Monteverdi's *Orfeo* is perhaps the first opera of real stature that is performed regularly throughout the world today.

Italy was where it all started. Corsi, Peri and Caccini were all resident in Florence and opera houses were soon set up in Mantua, Rome and Venice. Opera soon caught on all over the world, France being among the quickest to jump on the bandwagon with Jean-Baptiste Lully, the chief court composer to Louis XIV, providing the first offerings. England followed suit soon after and Germany and Austria gradually developed their own versions of operas as soon as the social and political climates allowed.

These early operas are of particular historic as well as artistic interest but they bear little relation to today's perception of opera by a public which has been stimulated by the recent performances of Pavarotti and co. We will therefore concentrate on what followed a little later. The subject matter of the serious eighteenth-century Italian opera such as Monteverdi's *Coronation of Poppea*, or Handel's *Julius Caesar*, was largely concerned with ancient tales of heroes and heroines. In contrast to these historic operas, categorized as *opera seria* (serious opera), there developed a more comic, fanciful style in *opera buffa*. The earliest forms of comic opera were usually very short and were often used as an interlude in the middle of an *opera seria* performance – a good example being *The Maid as Mistress* by Pergolesi, who was one of the foremost composers in Naples in the early eighteenth century. As time progressed opera grew more and more popular and nearly all of the great composers – Handel, Mozart, Beethoven, Puccini, Wagner and a host of others – became involved in writing such works.

The Italians consistently produced fine, attractive operas that gave full rein to the wonderfully agile voices of their singers. Rossini, Donizetti and Bellini immediately spring to mind as the leaders of the field, while Verdi, who came a little later, left an indelible mark on the history of opera by developing a unique dramatic style that influenced everyone who followed. Many people will, no doubt, be familiar with a number of arias from Mozart's operas that featured in the film *Amadeus*; later in the book we will take a close look at his role in the whole spectrum of opera.

The other major innovator and important figure in the overall development of opera is Richard Wagner. Famous for his *Ring* cycle, he brought to opera a new seriousness and intensity which abandoned pure musical display in favour of music that acts to heighten the dramatic content, the result of which is extremely powerful and, to some people's ears, quite shocking. Richard Strauss took things a stage further by creating brilliant colours of orchestral sound that had previously been missing even from the works of Wagner.

After delving into this period of 'mainstream opera', the works of the composers that we look at briefly in the *Where Next?* chapter include those of Richard Strauss, Stravinsky, Alban Berg, Shostakovich, Prokofiev, Benjamin Britten, Michael Tippett, Harrison Birtwistle, Philip Glass and John Adams, each of whom have made significant contributions to this glorious art-form.

Here follows a plain and simple introduction to the technical terms and key forms of opera that you're most likely to encounter, either in opera programmes or in the notes in CD booklets and record sleeves etc . . .

OPERA SERIA AND OPERA BUFFA

In the late seventeenth and the early part of the eighteenth centuries, *opera seria* (serious opera) was the term given to operas whose subject matters were largely concerned with ancient fables, historical tales, heroes and heroines. By way of contrast, and as something of a reaction to this rather formal way of dealing with the medium of opera, there came a fanciful, comic style which combined the elements of farce, intrigue and whimsicality. It grew up in eighteenth-century Italy and was known simply as *opera buffa* – the Italian for 'comic opera'. Rossini and Mozart were fine exponents of the latter and a couple of good examples are their respective works *The Barber of Seville* and *The Marriage of Figaro*, both of which focus on the antics of the colourful character Figaro.

GRAND OPERA

Over the years the definition has become slightly confused, but these days a reference to grand opera normally implies an opera on a large scale incorporating huge, extravagant sets and big crowd scenes (choruses). Verdi's *Aida* is a fine example and Mussorgsky's *Boris Godunov* also comes into this category.

CHAMBER OPERA

Smaller in scale than a regular opera, chamber opera is normally shorter and more intimate in nature. Such works were particularly popular in the immediate post-war years when there weren't the resources to stage grand full-scale operas. However, financial constraints had an entirely positive effect on the work of composers writing in this sphere and the resulting disciplines were put to good use in works such as Stravinsky's *The Rake's Progress* and Britten's *Turn of the Screw*.

OPERETTA

Short, light-hearted 'operas' that invariably include spoken dialogue, operettas are now almost synonymous with 'Musical Comedy'.

OVERTURE

Operas customarily begin with an orchestral overture which contains parts of the music that will follow later in the opera. Indeed, the Viennese composer Gluck stated that in his later operas the purpose of the overture was to prepare the audience for the plot of the play. Most other composers from the classical period concurred with this notion and by default overtures invariably contain some of the main highlights of the operas that follow, which is why many are now used as pieces to open classical music concerts. Good examples are to be found in the overtures to Mozart's *Marriage of Figaro* and *Don Giovanni* and Rossini's *The Barber of Seville*.

ARIA

The word *aria* is the Italian for 'air' – as in song. Usually in three sections, the first and third identical and the second section contrasting, there are a number of different styles of arias that originally applied to the early Italianate operas. In every case, one of the main purposes of arias was to show off the singers' prowess and vocal technique. The *aria cantabile* was always slow and smooth, allowing the singer freely to embellish the last section; whilst the *aria di bravura* or *aria d'agilita* display agility and skill and were by design very difficult to sing – Mozart's 'Queen of Night' from *The Magic Flute* is one of the most famous examples. The *aria parlante* ('speaking aria') was more 'telling' in its style and could be likened to a recitative (see later) and sung in an almost narrative style.

These are the main types of aria, but so involved was the whole business of writing opera in the early days that there are some thirteen other types of aria, details of which can be found in a good dictionary of music such as *The Oxford Companion To Music*.

An *arietta* or *arriette* is a smaller-scale version of an aria which can be described as a simple song-like piece.

CHORUS

The 'chorus' is the name given to the main body of ensemble singers who form the supporting cast in an opera. Usually the chorus comprises a combination of men and women, occasionally with groups of children. The members of the chorus, although anonymous in comparison with the solo operatic stars, are often called upon to sing many of the most famous extracts of the operas. Good examples are the 'Chorus of the Hebrew Slaves' from Verdi's *Nabucco* and the 'Sailors' Chorus' from Wagner's *Flying Dutchman*.

RECITATIVE

Recitatives in operas provide a style of writing that embodies an imitation of speech or narrative. Whereas arias are usually of a lyrical nature, recitatives often follow speech rhythms and take the place of straight dialogue that links the sections or arias and choruses.

There are two main types of recitative: *recitativo secco* (literally 'dry recitative') has a very simple accompaniment, usually played just on the harpsichord and perhaps the string bass element of the orchestra. Musically this type of recitative was quite fast-moving and declamatory in nature. In contrast, *recitativo stromentato* (instrumented recitative) has a full orchestral accompaniment and is musically far more complex and melodic.

BEL CANTO

This is the Italian term for, literally, 'beautiful singing'. It applies to a style in which the singer is required to deliver the solo line in the most even, pure and beautiful manner possible. *Bel canto* is commonly associated with the works of Bellini, Donizetti and Rossini, masterly composers of eminently singable melodies.

COLORATURA

In contrast to the flowing beauty of simple melodic lines in the *bel canto* style, coloratura passages demonstrate elaborate, highly decorated ornamentation of the melody. Sopranos are most commonly called upon to sing in this style, although there are these kinds of arias for male voices too. The best example of a coloratura aria is Mozart's 'Queen of Night' from *The Magic Flute*.

LEITMOTIV

Leitmotiv, the German for 'leading-theme', is the term applied to a special melody or phrase that is associated throughout a work with a particular character, situation or mood. The device is now most commonly applied to the music of Wagner, but he was not in fact the instigator of the practice. Even in some of the earliest operas – those by composers Monteverdi, Caccini and Peri, for instance – we find examples of such usage. Mozart, too, used the device with brilliant effect in *Don Giovanni*.

LIBRETTO

The libretto of an opera is the script or text to which the music is set by the composer. Sometimes the composer himself – Wagner, for example – wrote both the libretto and the musical score, but more often a specialist librettist or poet/playwright would write the text. Some of the most famous librettists include Lorenzo da Ponte (with whom Mozart worked closely), Francesco Maria Piave (Verdi's compatriot) and the celebrated team, Giuseppe Giacosa and Luigi Illica, who wrote the librettos for Puccini's *La Bohème* and *Madama Butterfly*.

THE VOICES

Singers of four main types appear in today's operas. In each type there are subtle differences that distinguish the quality and suitability of a voice to a particular style of writing or role:

Soprano

There are three distinct types of soprano voice and invariably it's the sopranos who are given the most popular arias in an opera. 'Dramatic sopranos' are identified by their histrionic quality and strong, powerful voices. 'Lyric sopranos', in contrast, have a particular lyrical quality that lends itself to more sustained and flowing melodic lines. The 'coloratura soprano' displays an agility and virtuosity of technique that requires a 'light' and flexible voice in order to master the brilliant but exceptionally difficult arias of the early Italianate composers.

Mezzo-soprano

This is the commoner of the two main types of female voice and is lower in register and quality than that of the soprano. Mezzo-sopranos rarely get the best roles in operas but there are, of course, a number of examples of superb repertoire including 'Non so più' from Mozart's *Marriage of Figaro*, sung by Cherubino.

Tenor

There are two main types of tenor voice. The *tenor robusto* has a full, strong character to the voice, eminently suitable for passionate, heroic roles, while the *tenor leggiero*, or 'lyric tenor', displays a more lyrical, smooth quality, rather like the lyric soprano. The tenor voice is lighter and higher in range than the other two male voice-types, baritone and bass. There is one other kind of 'tenor' voice, namely the 'counter-tenor'. This is sometimes referred to as the 'male alto' voice and can be likened to the adult male singing in falsetto – that is, as if the voice had not broken at adolescence.

Baritone and Bass

The baritone voice is generally regarded as being about a third higher in pitch than the bass and falls in the category of *basso cantante*, having a similiar quality to that of the lyric soprano and the lyric tenor as described above.

The *basso profundo* is the 'deep bass', the one that is used by composers for authoritative and powerful or solemn and melancholic roles.

CHAPTER TWO

Get Into Opera –
Your Starter Top Ten

The following ten excerpts from famous operas are a representative selection of the music of the composers who are acknowledged to number amongst the finest writers for the medium. Their work has, in most cases, been held in high esteem and remained genuinely popular for a hundred years or more. There are many other lesser-known and perhaps equally great examples that I could have chosen, but for our purposes here I have selected extracts that I feel will give the best introduction to the most popular styles. (Most extracts feature on the CD and cassette *Get Into Opera* – available at all good record shops and by mail order – see back of book.) There follows a short description of the piece in question – what opera it's from, who is singing and the background to the scene. In the next chapter we look in detail at the plot of each of the ten operas featured here, so that you'll be able to follow the story-lines. Then, whether you go along to experience the opera live, watch a video or listen to a recording, you will get the most out of the whole experience.

1 MOZART: *LE NOZZE DI FIGARO* (*THE MARRIAGE OF FIGARO*)

'*Porgi amor, qualche ristoro*' ('God of love, grant me some remedy')

Sung by the Countess Almaviva, the aria 'God of love, grant me some remedy', comes at the start of Act II when the complications of betrayed love, jealousy and mistaken identity are hotting up to fever pitch. One of Mozart's finest works, this opera contains a wealth of light, beautiful and immediately accessible music, and provides brilliant entertainment from start to finish.

2 ROSSINI: *IL BARBIERE DI SIVIGLIA* (*THE BARBER OF SEVILLE*)

Figaro Aria

This is undoubtedly the most famous aria from the opera, sung by the Barber himself, by way of introduction. Based on the same play by Beaumarchais as Mozart's *Marriage of Figaro*, this work is given a very different treatment by Rossini. It has become one of the most popular operas of all time for, as well as it being a highly entertaining story in its own right, here Rossini is at his very best with an endless series of 'show-stoppers' (such as this one) for all the singers involved.

3 DONIZETTI: *L'ELISIR D'AMORE* (*THE ELIXIR OF LOVE*)

'Una furtiva lagrima' ('A furtive tear')

Donizetti's opera about the spurious bottle of wine, which, it is claimed, is 'the elixir of love', is a highly engaging tale. Focusing on the potential love affair between Nemorino (a young farm labourer) and Adina (the rich, beautiful farm owner), this touching aria comes near the end of the opera just before Adina finally admits to loving her admirer. It's a beautiful aria, sung by Nemorino, with a very delicate accompaniment that demonstrates the incredible range and depth of Donizetti's talent.

4 VERDI: *AIDA*

'Celeste Aida' ('Celestial Aida')

Set in ancient Egypt, this opera follows the tale of two lovers who are parted because they are on opposing sides in a war. Radames, the Captain of the Egyptian Guard sings this passionate aria for the captured Ethiopian slave girl, Aida, with whom he is deeply in love. Taken from what is undoubtedly one of the grandest spectacles to be found in opera, this aria is a firm favourite with opera lovers and passionate tenors alike.

5 VERDI: *LA TRAVIATA*
(*THE WOMAN GONE ASTRAY*)

'*Libiamo, libiamo ne' lieti calici*'
('Let's drink, let's drink from the goblets of joy')

This is the famous drinking song (*Brindisi*) sung first by Alfredo, a young man who is besotted with the eccentric courtesan Violetta Valéry. After a while, Violetta, the host of the party and unaware she is the subject of Alfredo's desires, joins him in the song. One thing leads to another . . . and surprising antics of these and other equally colourful characters ensue, in this classic masterpiece by Verdi.

6 BIZET: *CARMEN*

'*L'amour est un oiseau rebelle*'
('Love is like a rebellious bird')

One of the most evocative and sensuous of arias from this magnificent opera set in Spain, it is sung by Carmen, the sexy young gypsy girl, to one of her many admirers. He is impatient to know when they can meet and, tantalizingly, she keeps him at arm's length by singing this, one of the most famous arias from the opera. The title means 'love is like a rebellious bird' – it won't come just when it's called!

7 WAGNER: *TANNHÄUSER*

The Pilgrims' Chorus

Wagner is undisputedly one of the greatest of all opera composers. This famous chorus comes at the start of a long epic tale, set against a background of medieval courtly life, that includes elements of ancient mythology. Full of symbolism and subtleties, this is a fine example that provides a taste of what is to come from Wagner's controversial pen.

8 PUCCINI: *LA BOHÈME* (*BOHEMIAN LIFE*)

'*Sì, mi chiamano Mimì*' ('Yes, I'm called Mimì')

A group of arty 'Bohemians' are the characters featured in this, one of Puccini's very finest operas. Rodolfo happens to meet Mimì, one of the neighbours, who has knocked on his door to ask for her candle to be relit. He gladly obliges and they fall in love at this first brief encounter, during the course of which he asks if he may know her name. She replies, 'Yes, I'm called Mimì,' and goes on to tell him about herself: although she makes a living embroidering artificial flowers, she has a real rose in her flat that will bloom in spring . . .

9 PUCCINI: *MADAMA BUTTERFLY*

'Un bel dì'
('One fine day')

This is the famous aria sung by Butterfly, a young Japanese girl who has married Lieutenant Pinkerton, a US Navy officer. After the joyful celebrations of their wedding, Pinkerton immediately has to set sail. Three years have passed and we are left wondering if he will ever return. Butterfly is the eternal optimist and sings that he will return . . . 'One fine day'.

10 GERSHWIN: *PORGY AND BESS*

'Summertime'

This is one of the first tunes that we hear at the start of the opera when it is sung by Clara as a lullaby to her baby. It's best known in the version sung by Bess later on, but has become a 'classic standard' that is sung by all types of singers in every style imaginable. Based on the novel by Edwin du Bose Heyward, *Porgy and Bess* is an opera set amongst the poor Black community in South Carolina. Full of jazzy inflections and colloquial language, this is a unique work that holds a special appeal for lovers of all kinds of music and it provides a most accessible vehicle with which to **Get Into Opera.**

CHAPTER THREE

The Composers And Their Operas

In this chapter we examine the composers and the specific operas featured in *Your Starter Top Ten*. A brief look at each composer's life and times (with more details for those which are particularly interesting or relevant) is followed by a synopsis of the opera, together with some suggestions for where to turn next if you're keen to pursue your particular interests.

MOZART: *LE NOZZE DI FIGARO* (The Marriage of Figaro)

Born in Salzburg, Austria on 27 January 1756, Wolfgang Amadeus Mozart died in Vienna at the young age of thirty-five. His life and times have been well documented and many will be familiar with the Peter Shaffer film *Amadeus* in which Mozart was portrayed as something of a hysterical genius. This may not be far off the mark, although we should never forget the uncommonly difficult circumstances in which the young composer found himself. Hailed as a *wunderkind*, he was paraded around like some sort of freak and the inevitable pressures this put on the young child must have taken their toll.

Undoubtedly some pressures he had to contend with were self-inflicted; others were due to everyday problems encountered in one shape or another by us all. It has always struck me, though, as being very unfair that he never found fortune in his own lifetime. A composer with his gifts and output living today would have an altogether different lifestyle. Nevertheless, it was Mozart's troublesome experiences that led to him writing the music that he did and for that we should be eternally grateful.

Mozart was a true genius and his works of extraordinary depth and beauty are a legacy for all to enjoy. He wrote some twenty operas and operettas and *The Marriage of Figaro*, which we will look at in detail now, is not only arguably the finest comic opera ever written, it is without doubt one of the most popular that is performed in opera houses all around the world. It is based on the well-known play by the Frenchman Beaumarchais and was the follow-up to another famous play, *The Barber of Seville*, which also has the character Figaro at its core. Both of these plays have achieved enormous success as operas: *The Barber of Seville* was originally set as an opera by Giovanni Paisiello (1740–1816) but has, of course, won mass popularity in the opera of the same name by Gioacchino Rossini (1792–1868) – more of which later.

Mozart teamed up with the librettist Lorenzo da Ponte for this opera. Da Ponte had already enjoyed some degree of success with other composers such as the infamous Salieri (Mozart's arch-rival as featured in the film *Amadeus*) and seemed a natural choice as the two got on very well and had much in common. The play by Beaumarchais was selected because the essence of the subject matter – masters and servants and their wildly complicated sexual relationships – is the very stuff of farce and invites thrilling, dramatic stage treatment. Mozart was so gifted at writing exquisite and 'witty' music, that when given a subject such as this – which he could really relate to – there was nothing to stop it becoming a true classic in every sense of the word. At the time that Mozart wrote the opera, the play was also politically relevant, which meant that the work was regarded as being something more than just a good farcical romp; indeed, its fast moving, effervescent and beautiful scoring make it a musical masterpiece in its own right.

The central character, Figaro, is the servant to Count Almaviva and is engaged to a beautiful young girl called Susanna, the maid to Rosina (the Countess Almaviva). The plot revolves around the Count's intention to exercise on Susanna the once customary 'feudal right' of the lord of the manor – that is, to steal a young girl's virginity before the husband-to-be takes possession. Sadly for the Count, this 'law' has recently been abolished on his estates and so he tries to follow another route in order to entice her into his life – much to the annoyance of the jealous Figaro.

Because the opera moves very quickly and there is a lot of recitative, it helps immensely to have a firm grasp of the way the plot develops, as otherwise one can easily get lost along the way.

Act I opens with Susanna and Figaro in their prospective bedroom. Susanna is trying on a hat and Figaro is measuring out the room for a bed. Susanna isn't at all happy with the room as it's so close to that of the Count, who, in her opinion, is quite definitely not to be trusted. Figaro tries to reassure her by saying that if the Count wants to 'dance', he shall dance to Figaro's tune. He leaves and an outrageous series of comings and goings take place following the entrance of Bartolo, the doctor. Bartolo has carried on a long-standing feud with Figaro and wants to get his own back, while Marcellina, Bartolo's former housekeeper, is jealous of Susanna as she herself is also passionate about Figaro. The two women sing a duet '*Via resta servita*' ('Accept my deference') and Marcellina eventually leaves politely.

Cherubino, the page, a role that is traditionally played by a woman with a soprano or mezzo-soprano voice, then enters the room. He's totally wrapped up in the idea of loving the Countess Almaviva, but his aria '*Non so più*' ('I no longer know') implies that he's really just in love with the idea of being in love – a common adolescent affliction. Cherubino shouldn't be in the room at all and, on hearing the Count's voice outside the door, hides behind a chair. The Count comes into the room and propositions Susanna, but, before he can get her to agree to a secret meeting, another voice is heard outside the door and the Count himself has to hide, for fear of being found alone with Susanna.

The music teacher Don Basilio enters and implies that he had heard rumour of an affair between Susanna and the Count, in the same breath mentioning Cherubino's desire for Rosina, the Countess. Basilio has long been a sort of uncle figure to everyone in the household, always keen to discuss their problems and offer advice. The scene at this point is really quite bizarre: Cherubino is hiding on top of a chair, covered by a dress, the Count himself is hiding behind it, and both are hearing everything that is going on.

The Count, no longer able to contain his anger, springs out from behind the chair. He says he's going to dispense with Cherubino and recounts the tale of an incident that had happened recently when he was visiting another young lady, Barbarina, where, on lifting up a cloth, he found Cherubino hiding. So saying, he lifts up the dress on the chair and finds Cherubino in exactly the same circumstances. Furious and embarrassed that the page must have overheard everything, he is understandably not appeased when Cherubino insists that he did his best not to eavesdrop.

Figaro arrives with a couple of peasants and, after presenting the Count with flowers, he boldly asks the Count to join Susanna and him in marriage. Finding himself put on the spot, the Count consents but skilfully avoids agreeing a date. He orders Cherubino out of the house and banishes him to life in the regiment. The Act then closes with a beautiful aria sung by Figaro, *'Non più andrai, farfallone amoroso'* ('No longer shall you go like an amorous butterfly'), who warns the page of the doom and gloom ahead.

Act II opens in the elaborate boudoir of the Countess, who sings an exquisite aria, *'Porgi amor, qualche ristoro'* ('God of love, grant me some remedy'), understandably upset that her husband, the philandering Count, no longer seems to love her. Susanna comes to see Rosina (the Countess) and tells of the problem that she herself is having: the Count is setting out to woo her. Cherubino arrives on the scene and sings one of the most famous arias from the opera, '*Voi che sapete che cosa è amor*' ('You who know what love is'). Rosina and Susanna hatch a brilliant plot to get their revenge on the Count: they decide to send him a note suggesting a secret meeting with Susanna, but instead of Susanna they will send Cherubino dressed up as a girl (remember that the part of Cherubino is played by a female).

The plan is destined for farcical confusion, but the two set to work straight away. They lock the door and start dressing up Cherubino, only to be disturbed by the sound of the Count outside. Another scene of concealment unfolds as Cherubino locks himself in the inner dressing-room and Susanna hides in an alcove. Rosina is clearly flustered when she lets in the Count who immediately senses something suspicious is going on. The Countess claims that it is merely her maid Susanna in the inner room, but the Count isn't inclined to believe her and he takes her away to find some tools with which to break the door down.

Immediately they leave, Susanna helps Cherubino escape out of the window and locks herself in the dressing-room in order to bear out what Rosina had said to her husband. The Count and Countess return and just as the Count is about to start forcing open the dressing-room door, Rosina confesses and asks for his forgiveness. The Count, fuming with anger, draws his sword and opens the door, only to find Susanna. Hurriedly the Countess 'covers up' by explaining that she had really only tried to shame the Count.

Now, when the tables are turned, the plot takes another twist as the gardener Antonio enters the scene moaning that someone jumped down from the window and ruined his plants. Figaro turns up and takes full responsibility for the damage but gets into an awful mess with his story when the gardener hands over the officer's commission which obviously was dropped by Cherubino. Then Bartolo and Basilio arrive with Marcellina, claiming that it is Figaro's duty to marry Marcellina on account of an unpaid debt! The chaos and confusion are only relieved by the curtain falling at the close of the Act.

The liaison between the Count and Susanna continues at the start of Act III with Susanna promising to meet the Count in the garden; but when the arranged time comes, the Count overhears Susanna talking to Figaro and sings an aria that questions why *he* should be unhappy at the expense of his servant. We then meet for the first time the Count's lawyer, Don Curzio, who, along with Marcellina and Bartolo, challenges Figaro about his legal obligation to marry Marcellina. Figaro thinks fast and offers the rather feeble excuse that because he is of noble birth he couldn't possibly marry anyone without the consent of his parents. In an attempt to substantiate his case he launches into a lengthy story, even offering to show them the fine clothes in which he was found as a child and the birthmark on his arm. Marcellina has the shock of her life on seeing this mark: she knows immediately that Figaro is in fact her long-lost son. This is not the only surprise, for she names Bartolo as the father!

What happens next is comically bizarre. The Count

storms about in a fuming rage, Figaro has an emotional embrace with his mother, upon witnessing which Susanna gets the wrong end of the stick and starts boxing Figaro's ears. The scene closes with Susanna, now in possession of the facts, singing the famous aria '*Sua madre? Suo padre?*' ('His mother? His father?'). The crowd disperses and we then focus on the Countess Rosina who is absorbed in recollections of the good times she'd previously enjoyed with her husband. She seems unable to think clearly about her predicament and can't decide whether she should be seeking revenge or trying to get back together with the Count, but eventually she resolves to ask Susanna to write to him (the 'Letter Duet'), thereby preparing the way for yet another trap of mistaken identity.

The next scene opens with a crowd of villagers visiting the Countess. Amongst them is Cherubino, in disguise. Revealed by Antonio, the gardener, Cherubino is once again in hot water and he is only spared with the assistance of Antonio's daughter, Barbarina, who has a hold over the Count. The nature of this is not clear but one's imagination is left to take a dim view of the Count. The celebrations then begin with Figaro leading the way for what turns out to be a double wedding ceremony. The two couples, Figaro and Susanna and Marcellina and Bartolo, arrive to seek the Count's blessing. During the course of the high-spirited dancing after the ceremony, Susanna secretly gives the Count the letter that the Countess and she had colluded over earlier and which they hope will lure the Count to a meeting, supposedly with Susanna but in reality with the Countess.

Act IV starts with Figaro coming across Barbarina in the garden. She had undertaken to return the pin that sealed the letter, so confirming the 'spurious meeting' between the Count and Susanna, but she has dropped it and is scrabbling around on the ground searching for it. Figaro thinks he has found out what is going on: Susanna is going to have a secret meeting with the Count. He's naturally absolutely livid with his new wife and, unable to think of a better plan, invites Bartolo and Basilio to be present at the scene of the 'crime'.

Figaro leaves, to be replaced on stage by the Countess and Susanna, both in disguise. Susanna is aware that Figaro is watching her and launches into a beautiful aria 'Deh vieni, non tardar' ('O come, do not delay'). What follows is quite the most intricate case of mistaken identity that one is ever likely to witness. Cherubino has also planned a meeting in the garden with Barbarina. He sees the Countess, whom he thinks is Susanna, and tries to kiss her, but the Count steps in and receives the kiss. The shock is too much and he lashes out at Cherubino, misses, and boxes by mistake the ears of Figaro, who has decided to take some action himself. The Count declares his love for 'Susanna' (it's really his wife!) and Figaro, in an attempt to get his own back on the Count, starts to unveil to the Countess (remember it's really his wife Susanna) what he thinks is the plot afoot. When Susanna forgets to alter her voice Figaro immediately catches on and changes tack by saying how much he loves her. This backfires on him as Susanna thinks that Figaro assumes he is talking to the Countess. However, Susanna soon realizes her mistake and in fun continues the charade in front of the Count. Figaro and Susanna start kissing and the Count, understandably indignant at this turn of events, is totally flummoxed when his wife reveals herself.

The tangled web of disguises now unravelled, the opera ends on a happy note with the whole company joining in the dancing and celebrations when the Count has made his peace with his wife. He has behaved abominably, but is forgiven by the Countess and the audience can, at last, relax after this uproarious last half-hour. There's not a dull moment in this, one of the most brilliantly constructed operas of all time.

The first performance of *The Marriage of Figaro* was given on 1 May 1786 in Vienna, with Mozart conducting from the keyboard. It met with such acclaim that the performance took almost twice as long as it should have done, the audience demanding most of the arias to be repeated as 'encores'. Despite this enthusiastic reception, after only nine performances the production was withdrawn as another opera had caught the imagination of those in Vienna: *Una cosa rara* ('A Rare Thing') by Martin. (This particular opera has not stood the test of time – indeed, only the most enthusiastic of opera buffs will even know of its existence.)

Since the luckless Mozart had received in advance a pretty derisory fee for composing this opera and it was withdrawn after only a few showings, he received no further payments. Mozart was, as usual, in dire financial straits and not only was he paying a high rent for his apartment but his wife was pregnant. She gave birth in October – only for the child to die, tragically, a month later. Paradoxically, this catalogue of disasters fanned the fire of Mozart's creative genius and he went on to write a succession of operatic masterpieces that nowadays form a very significant part of the established core repertoire for opera companies all around the world.

FURTHER RECOMMENDATIONS

Idomeneo: K.366 (*Idomeneus, King of Crete*)

Written in 1780, this is a fine example of *opera seria*. While it might not have quite the melodic appeal and comic charm of *The Marriage of Figaro*, it is well worth investigating. Giambattista Varesco wrote the libretto and the opera was first performed, one year after its completion, in Munich.

Don Giovanni: K.527

Written in 1787, this opera is often described as an *opera giocosa*, which is more akin to the *opera buffa* in that its subject matter is treated in a playful and high-spirited fashion. One of Mozart's finest operas, the adventures and eventual punishment of Don Juan (or Don Giovanni, as we now know him) make for some great entertainment. The librettist was the celebrated Lorenzo da Ponte and this two-act opera was first performed in Prague.

Così fan tutte: K.588 (*All Women are like this*)

Written in 1790, this is an example of *opera buffa* at its very best. The title doesn't translate adequately into English and has been known as 'Everyone's like this', 'The

School for Lovers', and 'Women's Ways', amongst others. The farcical, 'frothy' treatment that Mozart gives the opera can be interpreted in a more subtle and deep way if you so wish. However you care to appreciate the opera, Mozart's brilliant incisiveness in his handling of comic opera cannot fail to impress and entertain.

Die Zauberflöte: K.620 (*The Magic Flute*)

Written in 1791, this opera provides marvellous, almost pantomime-like entertainment. It contains such all-time operatic favourites as 'The Queen of Night' aria and the stammering aria 'Pa-pa-pa-pa-pa—geno!' *The Magic Flute* was written in German and first performed in Vienna, where it was an immediate success.

La clemenza di Tito: K.621 (*The Clemency of Titus*)

With this work, written in the year that he died, 1791, Mozart returned to the *opera seria* form and, though it is a beautifully crafted work, it appears that Mozart's heart was not really in it. Nevertheless, it was one of his most popular operas at the time and today is recommended for lovers of *opera seria*. Rumour has it that Mozart wrote most of the opera while travelling in a coach from Vienna to Prague. The libretto by Pietro Metastasio and Caterino Mazzolà was specified under the terms of the commission, and Mozart's dignified handling of the work is very much to be admired.

ROSSINI: *IL BARBIERE DI SIVIGLIA*
(The Barber of Seville)

Rossini's name is synonymous with opera. He was a master of his art, writing wonderful tunes in which audiences and singers alike delight. Although he went into voluntary retirement at the young age of thirty-seven, his legacy of music to the world of opera is considerable: in a nineteen-year span he wrote some thirty-six operas, of which the most famous are *The Barber of Seville, William Tell, The Thieving Magpie, The Italian Girl in Algiers, La Cenerentola (Cinderella)* and *Semiramide (Semiramis)*.

Gioacchino Rossini was born on 29 February 1792 in the beautiful Italian town of Pesaro and died aged seventy-six in France, where he had spent the last years of his life after suffering severe bouts of depression and various other mental health problems. The son of a municipal trumpeter, Rossini was an enormously gifted child. Both his parents were musical although his mother's singing engagements were somewhat sporadic. His father was fired from his job, as a result of airing his extraordinary political opinions, and this led to the young Rossini being sent to live with his aunt.

His interest in opera was evident from quite early on and his first efforts were so successful that he soon had a string of commissions to fulfil. The first full-length opera was *Tancredi*, true *opera seria* based on the tragedy by Voltaire. This was followed by the even more popular *L'Italiana in Algeri (The Italian Girl in Algiers)* which is a beautifully simple, frothy, light comic opera. These two works paved the way for his illustrious career. People delighted in the catchy tunes that he wrote and it's known that they used to go around humming and whistling his tunes in the street.

Riding on the tide of success, Rossini continued to compose quite prolifically. Many of these works do not attain the undisputed high standard of *The Barber of Seville* but most of them do get occasional airings at opera houses around the world. He was invited to Paris in 1824 and immediately set to work producing the French-language versions of his earlier *Maometto II (Le Siège de Corinthe)* and *Mosè (Moise)*, following which he composed a new one, *Le Comte Ory* in 1828. These all went down extremely well, but it was the larger-scale work *Guillaume Tell (William Tell)* that was to be the turning-point in his professional life. The opera, which was based on Schiller's play about the great Swiss hero William Tell and was his most developed work so far, proved to be the last thing of any significance that he wrote for many, many years.

Theories have abounded as to why he gave up serious composition – among them feature his habitual lethargy and love of socialising – his Saturday-night parties were infamous. Other than that, we know that he was disappointed by the mixed reviews of *William Tell*, that he was prone to intermittent patches of ill health and that he was still receiving a comfortable income from his previous works. Probably the reason for his winding down was a combination of all these factors.

The Barber of Seville is undoubtedly his finest triumph. It was originally made famous as an opera by the composer Giovanni Paisiello and this was the cause for some riotous scenes at the first performance of Rossini's version. The public at large thought it something of an affront to

Paisiello that another composer should produce a work on the same subject and with the very same name. However, once they had heard Rossini's wonderful score, the popularity of the original version faded rather quickly.

Like Mozart's *Marriage of Figaro*, *The Barber of Seville* is based upon a play by Beaumarchais, who had written a trilogy of plays featuring the central character Figaro. *The Barber of Seville* was the first in this series, *The Marriage of Figaro* the second, but, as yet, no-one has set the third play as an opera. The characters in Mozart's and Rossini's operas correspond, by and large, although chronologically Mozart's opera comes later in the sequence of events. The main difference in treatment of the two operas by the composers and their respective librettists (Rossini used Cesare Sterbini) is that in *The Barber of Seville* we never get the feeling there are any underlying political messages, that there is pathos or a comment on the 'serious' side of human emotions – jealousy in particular. Rossini's opera has a lighter touch. Bright, effervescent and vivacious, it provides sparkling, light-hearted entertainment from start to finish.

Synopsis of *Il Barbiere di Siviglia*

The opera opens in a noisy street scene where Fiorello, Count Almaviva's servant is conducting a band of musicians. The Count is singing the song '*Ecco ridente in cielo*' ('See, smiling in the heavens') underneath the window of a wealthy young lady, Rosina, who is under the charge of Dr Bartolo. Figaro, the barber-factotum of the city, makes a rather grand entrance and charmingly offers to help the Count get to know Rosina.

The beautiful Rosina comes out on to her balcony and drops a piece of paper into the street below. She claims that it is a piece of music that slipped out of her hand, but it's quite obviously intended for the attention of the crooner who had been avidly trying to attract her attention. The Count picks up the note and Rosina asks his name. Guardedly, for he does not wish Rosina to know his true identity (and station in life), he calls himself Lindoro.

Count Almaviva bribes Figaro to further his endeavours in the wooing of this young lady and they hatch a plan: Figaro will try to get the Count into the house by saying he's a drunken soldier in need of a place to stay. He seems confident that he can accomplish this and the scene closes with Figaro giving the Count directions to his barbershop, where they will meet later.

Next the scene shifts to a room inside Bartolo's house, where we see the strong-willed Rosina trying to get her way. She leaves and Bartolo tells his confidant Don Basilio, the music teacher, he's heard that Count Almaviva is in hot pursuit of the girl. In order to stem any further approaches, they decide to spread some evil rumours about the Count. Basilio sings the aria '*La calunnia*' ('The slander') in which we hear how a rumour can spread, be embellished and eventually reach such a magnitude that it will explode in a 'crash of thunder'.

In another room Figaro is having an intimate conversation with Rosina, telling her that Lindoro (the Count) is madly in love with her and he suggests that she write to him. Rosina, who, as has been hinted before, is of strong character and more than a little wily, has already prepared such a note. Bartolo is very concerned about the plight of this young girl. He marches into her room to insist that she behaves herself and never tries to deceive him. The whole scene changes as Lindoro, the 'drunken soldier', arrives. Rosina realizes immediately that this is her intended's way of infiltrating the household, but Bartolo, who is insulted that the drunk cannot even pronounce his name correctly, refuses the soldier the option of billeting.

There is a knock at the door and in come the police, wondering what all the noise and commotion is about. They are barraged with information from everyone in the room except Lindoro, whom an officer then arrests. The Count secretly reveals his true identity and the policeman clicks his heels, salutes and releases him, much to the amazement of everyone present. The scene draws to a close with all those who are not in the know expressing their bewilderment.

Act II starts with the arrival of a new character, a music master who claims to be standing in for the indisposed Don Basilio. This is, of course, the Count in another disguise, bent on another attempt to find his way to Rosina. He is so desperate to succeed that he even goes to the lengths of showing Bartolo the letter he has received from Rosina, hinting that there is intrigue here. In the famous 'Lesson Scene' Rosina sings, and, undoubtedly in the pursuit of learning, finds herself in close proximity with her teacher! The little episode that then follows has Bartolo trying to demonstrate his knowledge by explaining what 'good music' really is, but the scene changes with the arrival of Figaro who has a spurious appointment to shave the Doctor – obviously another ruse to pave the way for the Count to be alone with Rosina. This time it's foiled by the arrival of Basilio, who is quickly bribed (with a purse full of money) to go away, on the pretext that he is ill. In an aside we learn that the Count and Rosina plan to elope at midnight and that Figaro will help them on their way.

In the next scene we find out from Berta (an old maidservant) that one of the main reasons Bartolo is being so over-protective of Rosina is that he, too, is more than a little smitten with the young lady. Berta sings the aria *Il vecchiotto cerca moglie* ('The old man wants a wife') and it is clear that it is she who would wish to be *the wife*.

Bartolo then makes his first bold move and has a heart-to-heart chat with Rosina. He suggests that Figaro and the bogus music teacher are trying to lure her into the arms of another man – the illustrious Count Almaviva! Rosina is furious, convinced that she has been duped; she doesn't yet realize that Lindoro and Count Almaviva are one and the same person. She lets Bartolo in on the proposed plan to elope that night and in a wave of confusion agrees to marry the Doctor.

Figaro finds out about this and he and the Count arrive at the house. Amidst a very noisy scene they seize the opportunity to explain to Rosina all that has happened. Bartolo has, in the meantime, arranged for a notary to join Rosina and him in marriage, but the notary is persuaded to marry the Count and Rosina instead. Figaro and Basilio are the witnesses, although to join in the proceedings Basilio requires a little encouragement: a pistol held to his head. Bartolo arrives on the scene and is outraged at the turn of events. Intent on having Figaro and Lindoro arrested, he has brought with him a battery of officers and soldiers, but suddenly realizes what has actually happened. He retracts, comes to terms with the situation and then the opera closes with scenes of gay abandonment and merry-making.

Rossini was a great one for revamping bits of music that he'd written before for other purposes and then including them in later works: in this case he had used the overture to the opera in an earlier work and also one or two other extracts for various pieces. I don't think that this was because he was ever short of ideas, indeed, the opposite appears to be true in that he was incredibly prolific. In this and all of his other operas he displays a masterly talent for composing for the human voice: Rossini was supremely adept at writing 'singable' lines that not only sound wonderful and are extremely effective musically, but are also comfortably achievable for the singers concerned. Orchestrally, the music is colourful and very easy on the ear. The tunes are catchy and, once you've heard this music, there will undoubtedly be a number of melodies that lodge themselves enduringly in your memory.

FURTHER RECOMMENDATIONS

L'Italiana in Algeri (The Italian Girl in Algiers)

First performed in 1813, this is the opera that put Rossini in the forefront of the public eye. One of Rossini's most popular operas, it contains some of his most beautiful melodies and has a very catchy overture that is often performed at the start of many classical music concerts.

La Cenerentola (Cinderella)

First performed in 1817, this classic presentation of the fairy story *Cinderella* was, and remains, marvellous entertainment. Some amazing vocal pyrotechnics are accompanied by colourful orchestrations. Highly recommended.

Guillaume Tell (William Tell)

This magnificent, grand-scale opera is based on an ancient Swiss folk tale. *William Tell* was first performed in Paris, in 1829, and really marked the end of Rossini's days as a serious composer. The brilliant overture is one of the most popular of all time, frequently featured in symphony orchestra concerts and on compilation recordings of famous overtures.

DONIZETTI: *L'ELISIR D'AMORE*
(The Elixir of Love)

In the early nineteenth century Gaetano Donizetti (1797–1848) was one of the most popular operatic composers of his generation. He was born in the town of Bergamo, Italy, in 1797 and died there some fifty years later. Donizetti wrote numerous operas, of which *L'elisir d'amore* is the best known. Perhaps his most precious quality was that of being able to write superb melodies and embellishing them to show off the agility of the singers to their very best effect.

Audiences loved his work and he became a cult figure during his lifetime. Although he was acclaimed for his extraordinary flair for composing melodic, *bel canto* and virtuoso vocal lines, he stuck very much to the accepted practices of operatic style and form and so we don't remember him particularly as an innovator, more as a fine exponent of the nineteenth century opera that had developed. His music is similar in many ways to that of Rossini and Bellini and lovers of either of these composers will find similar enjoyment here, and vice versa.

During his career Donizetti composed over seventy operas, of which about ten are regularly performed today. Composing came easily to him, as can be seen from his prodigious output of completed large-scale works. He was well loved by audiences and critics alike and after the first performance of his *L'elisir d'amore*, at the opera house in Milan in 1832, he wrote enthusiastically to his former teacher, Mayr '. . . the *Gazzetta* review says too many good things; too many, believe me, too many!'

The libretto for Donizetti's *L'elisir d'amore* was written by the much respected Felice Romani, who also wrote for Rossini and Bellini with considerable success. The plot revolves round a bottle of wine, 'the elixir of love' that is given by a quack doctor to the hero, a simple village person, and we are involved in the charming tale of the effects that this bottle has on all who come into contact with it.

SYNOPSIS OF *L'ELISIR D'AMORE*

At the start of the opera the wealthy lady of the farm, the beautiful Adina, is seen reading her book about the two great lovers Tristan and Isolde. Trying to attract her attention is Nemorino, a young labourer, who is not having much luck in his attempts to win the lady's favour.

In fact, Adina's scornful response and her reading aloud from the book make him feel embarrassed and belittled. To his annoyance and further humiliation, Belcore, an army sergeant, arrives on the scene to pay court to Adina and we hear a trumpet playing a fanfare (off-stage) which signals the entrance of a splendid gold carriage. Out steps Dulcamara, a quack doctor, who immediately draws the curiosity of the assembled villagers with his extraordinary wares that he claims will be the answer to all their problems. Nemorino enquires if he has a potion such as the elixir that won the heart of Queen Isolde in Adina's story book, upon which the quack promptly produces an impressive-looking bottle that actually contains nothing more remarkable than red wine. The famous duet '*Obbligato*' ('Much obliged') then follows.

Satisfied and delighted that he has procured the means to gain the romantic attention of Adina, Nemorino settles down to a good meal. He knows the elixir takes only twenty-four hours to work and when Adina returns he coolly ignores her in a way that she finds quite irresistible . . .

Belcore, the sergeant, has received notice that he must leave with his detachment that very day. Impetuously he asks Adina to marry him right away, as he cannot bear to be parted without knowing of her love for him. In order to provoke jealousy in Nemorino, Adina appears to consent, which throws the young labourer into a frenzy – his elixir will not have time to work! Nemorino's repeated pleas to postpone the wedding by a day fall on deaf ears and the marriage plans proceed. All the other villagers are delighted at the prospect and we see busy scenes of their preparations for the forthcoming celebrations.

Act II opens at the farm, where the wedding feast has been set in readiness. The fiendish quack arrives with a new manuscript – a barcarolle from Venice that tells the story of a poor girl who rejects a wealthy old senator. Dulcamara sings with Adina a wonderful duet entitled '*Io son ricco, e tu sei bella*' ('I am rich, you are beautiful'). The crowd clap and cheer the two performers, then leave to watch the signing of the register, while Dulcamara stays greedily munching his way through the rest of the wedding fare.

We have not yet seen Nemorino in this Act and might be forgiven for thinking that the event will go ahead without him, but no: Nemorino comes in and sees Dulcamara, who being the sly trickster that he is, offers him another bottle of the magic elixir. This one, he claims, will work *instantly*. Nemorino does not have enough money to pay for the bottle and is thrown into a quandary. However, it transpires that Adina has delayed the signing of the marriage contract and, on seeing Belcore, Nemorino begs to join his regiment in order to be given the sum of twenty florins – the only way to lay his hands on some money immediately. Nemorino and Belcore then sing the popular duet '*Venti scudi*' ('Twenty florins').

Over now to a new scene, the village square, where we meet a country girl by the name of Giannetta, who breaks the news that Nemorino's uncle has died, leaving him a fortune. All the girls are now very interested in young Nemorino. He has quite a following of 'gold-diggers' and, unaware that he has become a very rich man, he puts down his sudden popularity to the consumption of this new magic elixir. In the next scene we see Adina in conversation with Dulcamara. She is deeply touched that

39

Nemorino has enlisted in order to raise the money to buy the elixir, but tells Dulcamara that she has no need for such a substance: women, she claims, have a potent elixir of their own. Dulcamara, obsequious as ever, agrees. At this point, Nemorino, who had disappeared with a crowd of village girls, returns. He notices the change in Adina's attitude towards him, has pangs of passion and sings a very moving aria, '*Una furtiva lagrima*' ('A furtive tear').

A lovely surprise then unfolds as Adina arrives back with Nemorino's discharge papers. She's bought him out of the army and she declares her love for him. Everything looks set to end on a highly romantic, happy note – which it does, although we see scenes of Belcore and his fellow-soldiers consoling themselves that there are plenty more fish in the sea. There's a nice twist to the tale which sees the opportunist Dulcamara doing excellent business, as all the villagers are convinced that it was the fake doctor's 'elixir of love' that had done the trick. What's more, the magic potion clearly brings money as well as love! The final scene is of the happy throng giving Dulcamara an exuberant farewell; his extravagant coach leaves and the curtain falls.

Donizetti's operas are engaging, tuneful and richly harmonic works. The solo voices, in particular, are always given marvellous opportunities for virtuoso display and Donizetti's imaginative handling of the writing for the orchestra is also singularly impressive.

Lucia di Lammermoor (*Lucy of Lammermoor*)

Based on the novel by Sir Walter Scott (*The Bride of Lammermoor*) and first performed in Naples in 1835, this tragic opera is regarded by many as Donizetti's finest operatic work. His coloratura soprano writing for Lucia, particularly in the 'mad scene', is among the most brilliant one is ever likely to hear.

Don Pasquale

First performed in Paris in 1843, this was Donizetti's last comic opera. It explored the well-worn plot of old men 'falling in love' with younger women and remains a huge success to this day. Donizetti wrote the libretto with Giovanni Ruffini, although it was originally attributed to Michele Accursi, in order to protect Ruffini who was living in political exile at the time.

VERDI: *AIDA* and *LA TRAVIATA*
(Aida *and* The Woman Gone Astray)

We have Verdi to thank for a major part of the central core of operatic repertoire performed in opera houses across the world today. Born on 10 October 1813 in the little village of Le Roncole, in the Italian province of Parma, Giuseppe Verdi was the son of an innkeeper. He was a naturally gifted child and showed such an aptitude for music that, at the age of ten, he was sent by his father to nearby Busseto, to concentrate solely on the study of music. He soon achieved success, composing music for the local Philharmonic Society as well as many pieces for the church, and although he was, by this time, too old to enter the Conservatorium in Milan he continued his studies with Vincenzo Lavigna, one of the conductors at La Scala – the most famous opera house in the world. His first serious offerings in the field of opera include *Oberto* (rarely performed today), followed by *Nabucco*, which was a huge hit at the time and has remained enormously popular to this day.

Verdi's life was marred by a number of devastating tragedies: both his children died very young and, when he was just twenty-five years old, his wife Margherita died of encephalitis. These grievous blows made him of a mind to give up writing music altogether. Fortunately a local impresario, Merelli, managed to persuade him to keep going and the next piece that Verdi wrote was the highly successful opera *Nabucco*, based on the biblical story of Nebuchadnezzar, King of Babylon.

Verdi's music is characterized by his extraordinary sense of drama. He has been described in the text books as the 'natural successor to Bellini and Donizetti'; while this may be true in the historic and chronological sense, Verdi brought a new, vital spark of drama and creative energy to opera that had until then largely been missing. He was prolific, writing steadily and, generally, consistently right up until the end of his life: *Otello* and *Falstaff*, two of his major operas, were composed when he was seventy-three and seventy-nine years old respectively.

Perhaps his most famous opera is *Aida*. Written over a two-year period starting in 1869, it was commissioned by the Khedive of Egypt and was first performed in Cairo, in 1871. The plot was conceived by the French Egypt-ologist A. E. Mariette and the libretto was written by Camille du Locle, in French prose that was subsequently translated into Italian and transcribed into verse by Antonio Ghislanzoni in collaboration with the composer himself.

SYNOPSIS OF *AIDA*

The opening scene is set in the royal palace at Memphis (the Egyptian setting is always presented in all pro-ductions with temples and pyramids and the like in the background). Ramfis, the high priest of Egypt, is the first to sing. He gives the news that their land has been invaded by the Ethiopians and tells Radames, the captain of the Egyptian guard, that the goddess Isis will declare who shall lead the Egyptian armies in revenge. Radames, hoping to be chosen for the part, imagines returning victorious to the palace in Memphis – and to his true love Aida. Here is the subject of great tragedy: Aida is the slave of Amneris (daughter of the King of Egypt), who is also smitten with Radames. Radames launches into one of the most popular arias from the opera, 'Celeste Aida', a tender and impassioned love-song. Amneris arrives and, seeing Radames in this joyous mood, quite rightly assumes that it can't have been occasioned merely by the prospect of pending military action. On recognizing the attraction Radames has for her slave, she is extremely jealous.

The king enters with Ramfis and an entourage of officers and is told of the damage that has already devastated the countryside and the possible threat to the capital city Thebes. The messenger mentions the name of the Ethiopian king, Amonasro, at which Aida cries '*Mio Padre!*' ('My father!'). The king announces that Radames has been chosen to lead the Egyptian troops who burst into a heroic song: '*Ritorna vincitor!*' ('Return Victorious!').

The scene ends with a moving episode in which the lonely figure of Aida is seen lamenting her predicament: she loves Radames but has strong feelings of loyalty both for her country and Amonasro, her father. As the Act draws to a close, at the Temple of Phtha, we see the ritual of the priests and priestesses presenting the consecrated arms and weaponry to Radames, who is gearing himself psychologically for the battle.

We don't see any of the fighting on stage, but the curtain opens on Act II with the news that the Egyptians have triumphed. Amneris is getting ready for the cele-bratory feast and her Moorish slaves are dancing for her. When Aida enters, Amneris, eager to find out if her suspicions have foundation, pretends all is well but then, in order to gauge her reaction, tells Aida that Radames has been killed in battle. Aida falls straight into the trap by confessing her love for Radames, only to be told that he is actually still alive. From a distance is heard the battle song of the returning soldiers and Aida is left on her own beseeching the pity of the gods in the touching aria '*Numi, pietà*' ('Pity me').

Next, at a temple near Thebes, is the most magnificent of the opera's famous spectacles – the Triumphal March (alternatively known as the Grand March), which accom-panies the entrance of the king, his soldiers and the dancing girls, together with resplendent chariots and idols. Radames is hailed a hero. Amneris places the victor's crown upon his head and the king promises he will honour any request as a tribute to his outstanding achievement.

The Ethiopian war prisoners are then brought on. Aida is shocked to spot her father amongst them, lurches forward and throws her arms round him. Amonasro quicky tells her not to reveal his true identity and, embarking on a cunning ploy, informs the Egyptian king that his Ethiopian counterpart has been killed. He begs that the lives of the other prisoners will be spared and is given the wholehearted support of Radames, who makes this his 'special request'. The king agrees, much to the disgust of his daughter Amneris and the assembled priests, but Ramfis insists that his daughter shall marry Radames. Aida and Radames are distraught and the Act closes with a brilliantly constructed scene of mixed emotions: high spirits and jubilation on the one hand and distress and sadness on the other.

Another temple is the setting for the opening of Act III. This time we are at the temple of Isis, close to the Nile. Chanting is heard from the priests and priestesses as Ramfis spiritually prepares Amneris for her wedding the following day. Aida has arranged a secret meeting with Radames, but before the war hero arrives there is another moving scene, during which Aida expresses her grief at the prospect of never returning to her homeland. Her father appears and says that she could go back safely if only Radames would divulge the intended path of the Egyptian soldiers, so that she could plan an alternative route. Aida is reluctant to press Radames on this point but, seeing her father's anger, finally agrees.

Radames eventually arrives and is totally beguiled by

Aida's charm. She makes him agree to go with her to Ethiopia and, just as they are about to set off, manages to extract the vital piece of information about the soldiers' proposed route. No sooner has Radames told her than we are taken by surprise by the sudden appearance of Amonasro, who at once reveals his true identity to Radames. As they are about to leave, the guards appear with Ramfis and Amneris, who have overheard the revelation. They try to arrest the Ethiopian king and a fight breaks out, but the brave Radames steps in, leaving an escape route for Aida and her father. For this great act of heroism Radames is imprisoned and the Act draws to a close on a note of high dramatic tension.

Not far from where Radames is to be tried for his crime, Amneris is alone in a room, grieving about the recent events. She loves Radames so much that she is prepared to do almost anything to save him. Amneris sends for her intended and promises to come to his rescue if he will agree never to see Aida again. Radames refuses point-blank and, although deeply upset, she heartlessly dispatches him to meet his fate. The trial takes place, Radames is proclaimed a traitor and is sentenced to be buried alive. He is about to be taken away when a grief-stricken Amneris bursts in.

The opera closes with the scene at the Temple of Phtha, below which we can see the crypt where Radames has been banished to spend his last days in a sealed tomb. Radames discovers that Aida has secretly hidden there and, as she falls into his arms and dies, the priests' and priestesses' chanting is once again heard in the distance, while Amneris prays for Radames' eternal peace.

★   ★   ★

The first performance of *La traviata* was given in Venice in 1853, when Verdi was forty years old. Surprisingly, for an opera that is nowadays recognized as one of the all-time classics, it was a complete disaster. The main reason for the failure was the overall direction and staging: the piece was originally set in the audience's own time and people found it hard to appreciate this contemporary background. Upon its initial demise, Verdi reset the opera in the time of Louis XIV, a period which suits the work well, and the opera has found considerable favour ever since.

This modification raises a very interesting issue: the 'treatment' and manner in which a particular opera is perceived and staged by a given director or company. Personal taste dictates whether one likes or dislikes a piece of music or theatre, but some directors these days have a penchant for doing something 'different' with the operas. There is, however, an enormous amount of evidence to support the point that traditional opera audiences like to see the operas staged as they were conceived by the composer. For my part, I'm all for experimentation and innovation, but I must say that contemporary settings invariably do little to enhance the original manuscript and concept in most people's eyes.

La traviata is based upon a play by Alexandre Dumas the younger entitled *La dame aux camélias* and the libretto is by Francesco Maria Piave, who altered the two central characters' names from Marguerite and Armand to Violetta and Alfredo in order to enhance the Italianate character of the opera. The strong cast of characters and the dramatic turns in the plot give rise to many highly charged and compelling scenes and this opera is now widely considered to be one of Verdi's finest.

Synopsis of *La traviata*
(*The Woman Gone Astray*)

Violetta Valéry, the central character in this opera is described as a courtesan – that is, a lady who is not a common prostitute but, rather, one who attaches herself socially to a succession of fashionable, well-to-do society men who support her opulent lifestyle. She lives in a lavish house in Paris, where the opening scene is of a party to which Violetta is welcoming her guests, among whom are Flora Bervoix (a close friend), Baron Douphol (an admirer), Viscount Gastone de Letorières (another friend) and Alfredo Germont. Gastone introduces Alfredo to Violetta as another man who has long admired her and she is flattered by this remark. As the party gets into swing, Alfredo is persuaded to lead the assembled guests in a high-spirited drinking song, or *brindisi* entitled '*Libiamo, libiamo ne' lieti calici*' ('Let's drink, let's drink from the goblets of joy') – a song that has become a popular classic. Violetta is so roused by the song that she, too, joins in and sings the second verse herself.

The party gathers pace and, when the ensemble of musicians strike up dance music, the guests make their way through to the dancing area in an adjoining room. Violetta, however, is struck by a coughing fit and a crowd of people, concerned and quick to comfort her, gather round. She sends them away to get on with the dancing, but, on looking into a mirror at her reflection, notices that all the guests but one have left her. It is Alfredo Germont who, in a tender moment, tells Violetta that he has been in love with her for a year. The scene is interrupted by Gastone calling from the other room and Violetta somewhat reluctantly sends Alfredo out. The party winds down and the guests eventually depart. Violetta, alone again, sings another classic aria, '*Ah! fors' è lui*' ('Ah, perhaps he is the one'), in which she thinks long and hard about the man she has met that evening – Alfredo. She goes through a fascinating thought process, musing on the new, 'pure' life she could lead with such a partner, before all but dismissing this prospect in favour of pursuing the delights of her social life (and all that goes with it). Still somewhat undecided, she gives a bold rendition of '*Sempre libera*' ('Ever free') reaffirming her desire to remain free.

Act II starts with something of a surprise for the audience. We are expecting Violetta to continue her life as before, but the first scene opens at a country house outside Paris where Alfredo and Violetta are now living. Alfredo, alone in the room, sings a joyous song about his new life: '*De' miei bollenti spiriti*' ('My turbulent spirits'). Annina, Violetta's maidservant, comes into the room and tells Alfredo that, on the instructions of her mistress, she has been to Paris to sell Violetta's possessions in an effort to clear their debts and support their opulent lifestyle. Upset and embarrassed by this, Alfredo hastily heads off for Paris to try to sort things out.

In the next scene, Violetta receives an invitation to a dance that evening from her old friend Flora. Suddenly, Alfredo's father enters the room. Giorgio Germont, an imposing figure, wastes no time in telling Violetta the purpose of his visit: it is to reprimand her severely for the financial ruin of his son. He is taken aback to find that it is Violetta herself who has suffered the consequences of their extravagance – that it is *she* who has sold off her precious belongings in order to rectify things. Giorgio then launches into the wonderful aria '*Pura siccome un angelo*' ('Pure as an angel') in which he asks Violetta to make a sacrifice on behalf of his daughter who may be facing the abandonment of her fiancé owing to Alfredo's apparent fall from grace. Giorgio asks Violetta to leave Alfredo without giving him a reason, and, after some discussion and many changes of heart, Violetta agrees – but only on the condition that Giorgio tells his daughter exactly what has happened.

Violetta quickly writes a note to Alfredo, telling him only (as she'd agreed with his father) that she has left him. Alfredo will know she has gone for good, and probably to another man. Giorgio is surprised and impressed by the way that Violetta has handled herself through this trauma and before he leaves he hugs her tenderly as a father might his daughter.

Violetta calls her maidservant Annina and, just as she is about to hand over the note for delivery, Alfredo enters the room and takes her by surprise. In a very tense and impassioned moment, Violetta asks Alfredo always to love her as she loves him and makes an emotional exit. Alfredo is totally bewildered until a messenger gives him Violetta's note, upon which his bafflement is flooded with grief. Coincidentally his father comes into the room and tries to console his distraught son. Giorgio suggests that they go back home, '*Di Provenza, il mar, il suol*' ('To Provence, the sea, the sun'), to restore Alfredo's spirits. However, Alfredo is jealously suspicious that Violetta has fled to

Douphol, a previous lover, and, on seeing the invitation she had received from Flora, decides that he will go to the party and have it out with Violetta.

The next scene is set at Flora's house where the party is in full swing. It's a party with a Spanish theme which provides an atmospheric and colourful flavour with Spanish music and guests in 'fancy dress' as matadors, gypsies and flamenco dancers. Alfredo enters and joins in a game of cards with a group of men and we see, across the room, the entrance of Violetta with the very gentleman Alfred suspects of wooing her away: Baron Douphol. Alfredo makes some insulting remarks which offend the Baron and a fight threatens to break out. Violetta, anxious to protect Alfredo, asks him to leave, but he will have nothing of it. He gets more and more angry and his fury reaches boiling point when Violetta tells him that she is in love with Douphol and that there's nothing he can do about it. This, of course, is just her way of avoiding telling Alfredo the truth, but it results in Alfredo calling the attention of all the other guests, throwing down his purse and declaring that he is now clear of all his debts. The guests are on Violetta's side and make their feelings known. At this moment Giorgio strides in and he, too, denounces the behaviour of his son. The Act closes on a heartrending scene where Violetta is faint and broken-hearted.

Another major time change has taken place with the opening of Act III. It is set in Violetta's new flat, where she lies in bed ravaged by consumption. Annina, her faithful servant, is still with her but Violetta has little money left and fate has been cruel. The doctor pays a visit and offers her reassurance and encouragement, but he warns Annina that Violetta has only a few hours to live. Violetta reads through a pile of letters, among which is one from Giorgio Germont telling her that he has confessed everything to Alfredo, who is now on his way to visit her in an effort to make amends. She sings a most beautiful aria at this point – '*Addio, del passato bei sogni ridenti*' ('Farewell, fair smiling dreams of the past') – in which she reflects on the past and all her vain hopes.

As we hear the sounds of the carnival outside the window Annina arrives back, bringing with her a visitor for Violetta. It is, of course, Alfredo and, as he falls into her arms, all the feelings of resentment and despair are banished for ever. He vows he will take her away to the country, but Violetta, overcome by excitement, feels drained and calls for help. When Annina leaves to fetch the doctor, Alfredo's father joins his son at the bedside. Violetta hands Alfredo a medallion, which she asks him to give to the girl he eventually marries. She is insistent, but all at once a serene mood returns and she reflects on the blissful time when she and Alfredo fell in love. The curtain closes after we witness her moving but peaceful death.

La traviata and *Aida* are probably Verdi's two greatest works but there are a host of others that are equally well worth exploring. A number of his works got him into trouble with the authorities, most notably *Rigoletto* and *Un ballo in maschera* ('A Masked Ball'), although *Macbeth, Nabucco* and *Aida* itself were also not without social and political messages to which many objected at the time.

The musical content of Verdi's operas all demonstrate his remarkable gift for writing great tunes: impassioned arias, for both male and female voices, abound and his ability to write stirring choruses has never been equalled. As his compositions developed and matured he created techniques for retaining thematic continuity; in the later operas one becomes totally absorbed in the drama of the piece while being subliminally affected by his subtle use of recurring musical themes. A perfect example of this is found in the last Act of *La traviata* when Alfredo returns to beg Violetta's forgiveness: Violetta hears the melody (played by the orchestra) that Alfredo sang when he first made his feelings known to her in Act I. Devices of this type were in existence long before Verdi started using them, but they had not been employed with such mastery. Wagner followed on from where Verdi left off in this respect, often taking things a step further by assigning a leitmotiv to a particular character, mood or, even, a political notion. This technique is particularly valuable for pieces on the grand scale of Wagner (and, to a slightly lesser extent, of Verdi) as it helps to provide the unifying factor that is so important in a long and complex work.

FURTHER RECOMMENDATIONS

Macbeth

Based on the Shakespeare play, this four-act historic opera, for which Francesco Maria Piave wrote the libretto, was first performed in Florence, in 1847. Verdi wasn't altogether satisfied with the end result, however, and in 1865 he revised the work for a Paris revival: it is this version that is most commonly performed these days.

Rigoletto

Written in the period between the first performances of *Macbeth* and *Il Trovatore*, *Rigoletto* was first staged in Venice, in 1851. Verdi had originally intended to call the opera *The Curse*, a reference to one of the main elements of the story-line, a curse laid upon a court jester. As one of the underlying themes attacked the very foundations of court life, Verdi fell foul of the censors, who banned his original draft of the work. *Rigoletto* contains the immortal favourite '*La donna è mobile*' ('Woman is fickle'), one of the most famous arias in all opera.

Il Trovatore (*The Troubadour*)

First performed in Rome, in 1853, this opera is full of wonderful, memorable tunes, including the 'Anvil Chorus', the 'Soldiers' Chorus', '*Di quella pira*' ('That funeral pyre's flames burn through me') and the duet '*Ai nostri monti*' ('To our mountains'), all of which feature in most 'operatic favourites' recordings. The romantic, historic plot is complicated but well worth taking the trouble to fathom. Salvatore Cammarano wrote the libretto and the opera is in four acts.

Other Verdi operas to move on to include *Simon Boccanegra* (1857; revised version, 1881), a powerful drama but more difficult to get to grips with because of the highly involved plot: Boccanegra was the ruler of Genoa in the fourteenth century and the opera follows the course of his personal and political fortunes until his murder some twenty-five years later.

La forza del destino (*The Force of Destiny*), written in 1862, is another complicated opera bursting with the traditional elements of a good plot – the fighting of duels, transvestism and eloping lovers. Among my other favourites are *Don Carlos* (1867) and *Otello* (1887), although neither of these measures up to the grand-scale spectacular provided by *Aida*, for example. *Un ballo in maschera* (A Masked Ball), 1859, also affords some wonderful moments but has never held mass popularity. It does, however, contain the beautiful aria '*Dì tu se fedele*' ('Say, have I been loyal'), which is another piece that frequently appears in operatic 'highlights' compilation recordings.

Verdi's last opera was the three-act comic opera *Falstaff* (1893). It seems rather strange that, after a succession of tragic operas, Verdi should draw his operatic career to a close with a comedy, but both this opera and *Otello* were inspired by the works of Shakespeare. *Falstaff* was actually based on *The Merry Wives of Windsor*, although included is a scene culled from *Henry IV, Part I* (the 'Honour Monologue'). For both of these Shakespearian operas Verdi used the librettist Arrigo Boito, himself a fine composer, who wrote the exquisite but rarely performed opera *Mefistofele*.

BIZET: *CARMEN*

Georges Bizet was born into a very musical family in Paris, on 25 October 1838. Not surprisingly he showed a precocious gift for music: he was a brilliant pianist and started composing at a very young age.

After an initial flurry of success winning various prizes

and awards, his career as a composer was never very settled. Bizet's first attempt at writing an opera, *La Guzla de l'Emir*, was withdrawn before it ever saw the light of day, as was *Ivan the Terrible* some years later. It appears he had a number of ethical and philosophical problems, with which he failed to come to terms and there is much documented correspondence throwing light on his moral dilemma. On the one hand he had strong ambitions musically and on the other he was cursed with a naïve cynicism, as a result of which his development as a composer was impaired and the flow of his creative thought processes was curbed.

Other than the opera *Carmen*, only a handful of his works now achieves regular performance on the concert platform. From his other well-known opera *Les pêcheurs de perles* ('The Pearl Fishers'), only the big duet stands out above the rest of the material, while his *Symphony in C* is a firm favourite, as are the hauntingly beautiful songs '*Nuits d'été*' ('Summer nights'). The two *L'Arlesienne* suites incorporating the catchy '*Farandole*' are tremendously popular and many will recognize the twelve pieces for piano duet entitled '*Jeux d'enfants*' ('Children's games'). Bizet's compositional career took some time to get going and was tragically cut short when he died in 1875 of a highly developed throat infection.

The opera *Carmen* was written right at the end of Bizet's short life and was first performed in Paris, in 1875. It's based on the book of the same name by Prosper Mérimée and the superb libretto was written by two other French writers, Henri Meilhac and Ludovic Halévy. Set in Seville in the 1820s, the opera never fails to conjure up evocative images of the time and Bizet's characterization of the gypsy girls and the toreador have led to the well-known stereotypes of such characters today. Amazingly *Carmen* received a frosty reception from the critics, who were shocked by the work, but Tchaikovsky, one of Bizet's contemporaries, declared that in ten years' time it would be the most popular opera in the whole world.

The great man's prophecy was not far short of the mark, for audiences then, as now, found the plot gripping and the music intensely dramatic. Containing as it does many tunes with which we are all familiar, *Carmen* ranks highly amongst recommendations for a first-time visit to the opera.

SYNOPSIS OF *CARMEN*

The opera opens on the bustling town square of Seville, in southern Spain. At one side of the square is a guard-house surrounded by a crowd of soldiers and on the other, a tobacco factory. Morales, a corporal who is clearly the ringleader of the soldiers, rouses his colleagues into song as they idly watch the world go by. A pretty peasant girl asks Morales if he knows another corporal, her childhood sweetheart Don José. He tells her she will have to wait until the guard changes before José will come and, in the meantime, engages in a flirting game with the innocent young girl.

A trumpet fanfare announces the changing of the guard and children in the square sing delightedly as the spectacle takes place. Morales tells José that a young girl has been enquiring after him and a conversation follows between a lieutenant, Zuniga, and José about all the charming girls who work at the cigarette factory. José isn't really interested in any of this as he has eyes only for Micaela, his sweetheart.

When a bell signals the end of the day for the factory workers the girls come out, much to the satisfaction of the ogling soldiers. There are exchanges of banter between the men and the girls, but our eyes are drawn to the very last girl to walk out of the factory gates – a beautiful, sexy, gypsy girl called Carmen, who is to command our attention for the rest of the opera. She sings at this point one of the most famous of operatic arias, the habanera '*L'amour est un oiseau rebelle*' ('Love is like a rebellious bird'), and with this she captivates all the soldiers gathered round – all except one, José, to whom she provocatively throws a flower before going back into the factory.

A disconcerted José is met by Micaela, who hands him a letter from his mother. They sing a duet, '*Parle-moi de ma mère*' ('Tell me about my mother'), an enchanting song in which the two remember fondly their village life back at home. When Micaela leaves, José reads the letter and we see that he's torn between his sense of loyalty and his strong desire for Carmen.

The scene is shattered by sudden shouting and screaming from the factory. A number of girls rush out and we learn that there has been an incident involving the beautiful seductress Carmen. José is sent to investigate the carry-on and he brings out Carmen, who is required to answer to Zuniga. She scorns him, singing 'Tra-la-la!' in response to his questions, and when Zuniga learns she has made a knife attack on one of the other girls he sends her off to prison.

It falls on José to take Carmen away and, while they are alone, she tries to seduce him. He tells her she must not speak to him and so, in an effort to continue her provocative behaviour, she sings 'to herself'. So alluring is her manner that soon José is bewitched by her charms. She promises to give him her love at Lillas Pastia's inn and anticipation breaks José's resolve: he loosens the rope that binds her wrists. Zuniga comes back with a warrant and just as José is leading Carmen away, she pushes him (as they had arranged) and scurries off.

Act II is set some two months later, at the inn where Carmen had promised to wait for José. There's a lively atmosphere in the bar and folk are singing and dancing. When Carmen has sung '*Les tringles des sistres tintaient*' ('The guitar strings were ringing'), Zuniga, who is also at the inn, tries to take Carmen away with him. She rejects his advances but in the course of the conversation learns that José has just been released from prison, where he had been kept since allowing her to escape.

Escamillo, a famous toreador (bullfighter), flamboyantly enters the tavern. He sings his famous aria '*Votre toast!*' ('Your toast!') and is cheered along by the crowd. After Escamillo makes an unsuccessful 'pass' at Carmen the drama gradually winds down and the crowds disperse, leaving Carmen with two other gypsy girls, Mercedes and Frasquita.

A couple of smugglers, El Dancairo and El Remendado, arrive at the inn and ask the gypsy girls for help. They have some sort of plan in which they try to involve the three girls, but Carmen, intent on keeping her assignation with José, refuses to oblige. The smugglers leave, but only after she has agreed to try to persuade José to meet up with them later. Then José comes and she is overjoyed. He tells her that he loves her and she dances for him, only to be interrupted by the sound of a bugle summoning the soldiers. José gets ready to leave, but Carmen is enraged that their romantic reunion can be ruined by a mere bugle-call! José hastens to tell her how much he has missed her and, in the famous Flower Song – '*La fleur que tu m'avais jetée*' ('The flower you threw to me') – how he has kept the beautiful flower she tossed to him the day he was imprisoned. Not one to give up easily, Carmen tries to entice him to stay by enthusing about the free life they could share together up in the mountains with the gypsies and smugglers. José is sorely tempted but the call of duty is strong.

As again he prepares to leave, there is a knock at the door and Lieutenant Zuniga makes a dramatic entrance. Clearly very smitten by Carmen, on seeing José he asks her if she would rather choose a common soldier than an officer. He orders José to return to the camp, whereupon José draws his sword. A duel is about to start, when the smugglers (who had been hiding) overpower Zuniga. José, his army career abruptly ended, joins in a rousing chorus, joyously extolling the virtues of his new 'free life' with Carmen.

Act III opens on a very different scene. Up in the mountains the smugglers are hatching their plan. Carmen is fed up with José's jealousy and he, in turn, seems to be dissatisfied with his new life after all. She suggests that he should leave them, but José is defiant and jealous and an angry scene erupts. When this finally blows over and the men settle down for the night, Carmen, Frasquita and Mercedes read their fortunes in the Tarot cards. Carmen's forewarn of her death . . . and then José's, too.

One of the most dramatic scenes in the opera then

follows as the smugglers and the gypsy girls go off to carry out the 'master-plan'. José is left behind but the stage is empty at this point, when Micaela appears. Her unexpected arrival is quite a shock to the audience, many of whom will have forgotten about her. She has paid a guide to bring her to the smugglers' den in the mountains and here she glimpses José, but a gunshot rings out. Micaela takes cover and realizes that it was José who had shot at a figure in the distance. He had missed but we find that the intended victim is the toreador Escamillo, who has been rounding up bulls for the next fight. He explains that he has also come to find Carmen, having heard she was no longer enchanted with her latest lover. José, as we already know, is a jealous man and when Escamillo delivers the line 'her [Carmen's] affairs last only six months', he cannot contain himself and in the presence of Micaela he draws his sword on Escamillo and they fight.

Carmen returns with the smugglers just as José is about to deliver the final blow. She grabs his arm and stops him stabbing Escamillo. The smugglers have to restrain José as Escamillo leaves, but at that moment one of them finds Micaela, who has hidden. She begs José to come away with her, but José announces histrionically that only death will part him from Carmen. Carmen and the smugglers then also try to persuade him to go, but it is only when Micaela says that his mother is on her deathbed that he gives in. As he prepares to leave he tells Carmen that they will surely meet again. She hears Escamillo's voice and makes to follow him, but José forces her to remain.

At the beginning of Act IV the action has shifted back to the town square in Seville. A large crowd is gathering outside the amphitheatre where a bullfight is to take place. The procession of those taking part in the fight arrives and Escamillo is greeted as a hero by the crowd. He shares in a short flirtatious love-duet with Carmen and then leaves to get ready for the fight. Frasquita and Mercedes warn Carmen that they have seen José in the crowd and advise her to be extremely careful.

Sure enough, José manages to find Carmen and he tries to win her back. She tells him she can't forget the past and that her love for him is dead. A great cheer hailing Escamillo roars from the stadium and Carmen moves towards it, but the distraught José violently bars her way. She gives him the option to kill her or let her go to see her new love and, when José responds angrily, she throws his ring at him and tries to dodge past. He catches hold of her and stabs a knife into her back. We hear the sound of the crowd singing the *Toreador's Song* as, fatally wounded, Carmen falls to the ground.

The final scene is of the devastated, pathetic figure of José, kneeling beside his former lover's dead body. He gives himself up to the authorities and the final curtain comes down.

FURTHER RECOMMENDATIONS

Although Bizet wrote a number of other operas, the most famous of which is *Les pêcheurs de perles*, they are less well known and, in some cases, now largely neglected. These include: *Ivan the Terrible, The Fair Maid of Perth*, and *Djamileh*. However, these operatic works are not of the calibre of *Carmen*.

The fascinating and controversial character Richard Wagner changed the face of opera for all who followed in his wake. Never before had anyone tackled subjects so fantastic and intense, incorporating all aspects of politics, sociology and moral philosophy. Of course, he had to formulate a new kind of musical and operatic architecture in which to encapsulate his creative ideas and these are best demonstrated in his most famous work *Der Ring des Nibelungen* (The Nibelung's Ring) – a cycle of operas incorporating four operas: *Das Rheingold* (*The Rhine Gold*), *Die Walküre* (*The Valkyrie*), *Siegfried* and *Götterdämmerung* (*Twilight of the Gods*). *The Ring*, as this group of operas is most commonly known, was first performed in its entirety (it takes more than three days) at Wagner's own theatre in Bayreuth in 1876.

Richard Wagner was born in Leipzig on 22 May 1813. His father was probably the actor Ludwig Geyer, whom his mother married a year later, after the death of her husband. Having a theatrical background, Geyer naturally encouraged the young boy's interest in music and drama and Wagner became quite proficient on the piano and took lessons in composition with the sole intent of providing incidental music for the theatre. He was obsessed with this aspiration, but still it came as a shock to his parents when they discovered one day that their son had not been to school for some months: he had been in hiding and totally absorbed by his compositional work.

He went to the university in Leipzig in 1831, aged eighteen, but showed little interest in academic work, being far happier socializing and contributing to in-depth discussions at the debating society. Wagner's passion was undoubtedly music, but his early compositions met with mixed reactions. His first efforts at writing opera were *Die Hochzeit* (*The Wedding*) – which was left uncompleted – and *Die Feen* (*The Fairies*), also based on his own libretto. In 1815 his brother Albert got him a job at the theatre in Würzburg where he fell in love with a young actress named Minna Planer, whom he later married.

Wagner was hopeless at managing money and he and his wife soon found themselves in financial difficulty. They fled the debts they had run up in Magdeburg (his next engagement after Würzburg) and promptly went on to do the same in Königsburg. Minna had eventually found a job there, but the money she earned soon disappeared; ashamed and despairing, Minna left Wagner and went home to her parents in Dresden, only to be followed by her husband. He managed to patch things up, got the job as Director of Music in Riga, and for a time their life became more settled, but in 1839 Wagner was given the sack. In order to escape another battle with numerous creditors, they smuggled aboard a ship bound for London. Terrible storms blew the ship off course and they found themselves in a Norwegian fiord, where Wagner gained the inspiration for his opera *Der fliegende Holländer* (*The Flying Dutchman*). The couple finally arrived in London, stayed at an inn in Soho and then went on to Paris.

Having made the acquaintance of two well-connected elderly Jewish ladies on the steamer between England and France, Wagner was introduced to Meyerbeer, the celebrated composer of the time who in turn introduced him to various luminaries of the Parisian music scene.

However, once again Wagner fell into debt and, though he was lent money from 'friends', he wound up in prison, penniless.

Mixed fortunes followed his release. The opera house in Dresden put on a number of his operas, including *Rienzi*, *The Flying Dutchman* and, later, *Tannhäuser* (which we look at in detail in the following pages). Sadly, these triumphs failed to set to rights his finances and, when they progressed from bad to worse, a warrant went out for his arrest, forcing him into political exile in Switzerland.

Wagner spent much of his time in Zurich writing essays and conducting an affair with the young English wife of a wine-merchant, before launching himself into writing the *Ring* cycle. A wealthy silk merchant took a shine to Wagner and gave him and Minna a place to live, where-upon Wagner managed to complicate his life still further by having an affair with the wife of his benefactor! It was not a wise move, but some good did result: the affair inspired him to write the wonderfully romantic opera *Tristan und Isolde*, which has been a firm favourite with opera lovers ever since.

Following the inevitable break-up of his marriage and Minna's return to Dresden, Wagner became involved with Cosima von Bülow, wife of the celebrated conductor Hans von Bülow and illegitimate daughter of Franz Liszt. Cosima had Wagner's child but Hans treated the child as his own. The intricacies of Wagner's life were further complicated when he became very close to the homosexual monarch Ludwig II, the King of Bavaria – although it would be quite wrong to imply that Wagner, himself, was gay. This friendship was considered an absolute

65

outrage by everyone and Ludwig, who accepted Wagner's relationship with Cosima, paid for Wagner to live with Cosima in a villa on Lake Lucerne.

Shortly after this Wagner wrote *Die Meistersinger von Nürnberg* which, in some people's view, is notorious for its references to the very strongest aspects of nationalism – whilst Wagner claimed it extolled the spirit and prowess of his nation. The following year Cosima gave birth to Wagner's third child. She got her divorce from Hans von Bülow and the two lovers were eventually married. King Ludwig, still infatuated with Wagner, continued to support him and it was with his help that Wagner set up his own theatre just outside Bayreuth, which is still in use today for performances of the great composer's works. The *Ring* cycle was the first work to be performed there, after which he composed another significant opera, *Parsifal*. The Wagners headed off to Venice for a break after the first night of *Parsifal* and it was there that Richard Wagner died of a heart attack on 13 February 1883.

SYNOPSIS OF *TANNHÄUSER*

The opera is based on the legend of the Venusberg – a hill within which Venus, the goddess of love, corrupted the souls of men with whom she came into contact. This is linked to the other main strand of the plot, a singing contest, which in itself provides terrific scope for an operatic composer.

Act I opens inside the Venusberg and we see scenes of lovers taking pleasure in various erotic acts (according to the discretion of the director!). Tannhäuser is resting his head on Venus's lap and morosely confesses dissatisfaction with his decadent life of the past year. She comforts him and asks him to sing for her, and he obliges with '*Dir töne Lob*' ('Praise resound to thee'). His determination to leave, however, upsets Venus greatly. She begs him to stay, but when he refuses she becomes angry and orders him to go, adding that there will be no salvation for him. He replies that his hopes rest in the Virgin, but, at the very mention of the name, Venus and the Venusberg disappear.

We then see Tannhäuser in a completely different situation – a valley near the Wartburg river, where a shepherd boy is playing his pipe and a crowd of pilgrims chants. On hearing the shepherd boy wish the pilgrims Godspeed, Tannhäuser falls to his knees and prays. As the pilgrims move out of view, we hear the sounds of approaching huntsmen – the Landgrave (monarch) of Thuringia and five minstrel knights.

The Landgrave and two knights fail to recognize Tannhäuser until a third one, Wolfram, realizes who he is. An enthusiastic greeting ceremony follows and the Landgrave and all the knights try to persuade Tannhäuser to rejoin their troop.

Tannhäuser resists – he feels he cannot go back with them now, after all his dissolute adventures – but eventually succumbs when Wolfram tells him that Elisabeth (the Landgrave's niece) is in love with him. The Act closes with all joining in jubilant song.

Act II opens with Elisabeth singing '*Dich, teure Halle*' ('To you, O hall of song'), sometimes referred to as 'Elisabeth's Greeting'. She is in the Minstrels' Hall and Wolfram enters with Tannhäuser, who flings himself at her feet. Elisabeth asks what has happened to him in the long time that he has been away but gets a very sketchy answer. They join in a beautiful love duet, during which an aside from Wolfram reveals that he has always been in love with Elisabeth himself. It is a painful moment for the knight who has enticed his rival back.

Wolfram and Tannhäuser leave and are replaced by the Landgrave, who greets his niece. Then trumpet fanfares herald the arrival of guests for a singing contest of the minstrel knights. The choral march 'Freudig begrüssen wir' ('Joyfully we greet') accompanies the noblemen and their ladies, the spectators of the great event. The competing minstrels enter the hall and the Landgrave announces that the theme of this competition is to be Love.

Each minstrel's name, inscribed upon a piece of paper, is placed in a special cup. Elisabeth has the honour of drawing the names from the cup. The first contestant is Wolfram, who stands and, accompanied by a solo harp, sings a plaintive, simple song about the purity of love. His rendition suggests that it is inspired by the very lady who drew his name from the cup. Wolfram finishes his song and Tannhäuser interrupts the crowd's approving response with suggestive comments on the more passionate aspects of love.

The next contestant is Walther and, like Wolfram, he sings a beautiful idealistic song focusing on the purity of love. This time, Tannhäuser shocks the crowd by loudly singing of lust and love's fulfilment. There is uproar at this and Biterolf challenges Tannhäuser to a duel. The Landgrave and Wolfram step in to calm them down but then Tannhäuser breaks into song again (the one celebrating the goddess of love, Venus, that we had heard in Act I). Never before has there been such an outrage at a competition. The ladies of the audience leave in disgust and the minstrels crowd round Tannhäuser in a menacing manner. Elisabeth stands protectively before Tannhäuser and, with urgent pleas, manages to persuade them to spare him.

Tannhäuser prays for forgiveness, at which point the Landgrave authoritatively takes centre stage and announces that if Tannhäuser is to be spared he must join the next group of pilgrims going to Rome, to seek absolution from the Pope. Everyone, agreeing, shouts 'Nach Rom!' ('To Rome!') and threatens Tannhäuser with death if he will not comply with this resolution. Tannhäuser races off to join the Pilgrims, whom we can hear in the distance.

Elisabeth is seen at prayer at the start of Act III. She is kneeling before a shrine in the valley by the Wartburg river and, still deeply in love with Tannhäuser, she prays for his forgiveness and return. We see Wolfram looking on and hear the chanting of the approaching pilgrims. Elisabeth and Wolfram watch as the pilgrims pass by – but Tannhäuser is not among them. Elisabeth, deeply distressed, falls to her knees to pray again and spurns Wolfram's offer to stay with her by way of comfort. Eventually she leaves and, as darkness falls, Wolfram sings and plays his harp. He is just coming to the end of his song about 'the gracious evening star' (undoubtedly inspired by Elisabeth) when Tannhäuser, tattered and drooping with weariness, arrives unexpectedly. In view of the angry scenes that accompanied his exit from the singing competition, Tannhäuser thinks that Wolfram will still be hostile but, touched instead by the warmth and kindness that Wolfram shows, he tells him of the trials and tribulations that he's encountered on his pilgrimage.

He failed to be absolved by the Pope – forgiveness was as 'likely' as the Pope's crook bursting into flower – and now he has decided to go back to Venus.

The most fantastic and extraordinary scene then follows when Tannhäuser cries out for Venus: visions of her appear and we hear her voice. As Wolfram tries to restrain Tannhäuser he mentions Elisabeth's name. Tannhäuser, as if suddenly struck by a magic spell, repeats the name over and over again; then, out of the blue, a solemn procession marches dolefully past. It is the funeral of Elisabeth and all the characters in the opera are part of the cortège. The apparition of Venus disappears as she cries '*Mir verloren*' ('Lost to me!') and Wolfram tells Tannhäuser that he is finally absolved. Relieved but distraught, Tannhäuser is led over to the coffin stand, where he falls to the ground and dies.

As the next day dawns, another group of pilgrims arrives. They are in high spirits, proclaiming that a miracle has occurred: the Pope's crook has burst into flower. This, they are certain, is a sign from God that Tannhäuser is now saved. The assembled company praise God with a rousing chorus.

The first performance of *Tannhäuser* was given in Dresden in 1846, the year after Wagner had finished work on the opera. A revised version with three fundamental changes was performed in Paris some fifteen years later, Wagner having by then changed his opinions on various matters of scoring and structure. Both the original work and the later one, which is known as the 'Paris Version', are performed these days, at the discretion of the directors and producers involved.

In this, one of Wagner's more accessible operas, we see almost the whole gamut of devices that he uses so brilliantly in his construction and composition of the music. The overture, for example, embraces all the thematic motifs that will appear later in the opera and so, through this relatively short first segment of the work, one can follow the whole sequence of events as they are depicted musically.

Most of the characters and story-lines have a theme or themes (leitmotivs, as Wagner named them) to identify themselves. Far from complicating the issue, this musical device helps to give unity and to draw the listener into the plot. The technique has been used in various musical forms ever since. John Williams, one of the current composers of film scores, applied it with particularly dramatic effect in the *Jaws* movies: every time the shark is about to appear, the haunting, menacing motif strikes up and we know that danger lurks nearby. The use of leitmotivs, by Wagner and others, works splendidly to provide coherency in a large-scale musical work that could otherwise become so complicated as to be in-comprehensible.

Wagner wrote many operas, all of them on a grand scale. Their subject matter and the style in which the music is written are not the easiest to get to grips with, but, as with a lot of music, the fact that an opera may take a few hearings to be really appreciated shouldn't dissuade one from exploring it. People tend either to love or loathe Wagner – perhaps in the same way that some find the literary works of Tolkien absolutely fascinating, while to others they are not in the least bit appealing. Whatever your personal tastes, though, I do urge you to try some of Wagner's work, starting off with *Tannhäuser* and then moving on to *Tristan und Isolde* or *Der fliegende Holländer* (*The Flying Dutchman*) before exploring the *Ring* cycle. It's marvellous stuff and, once you're into it, you'll be hooked for life.

FURTHER RECOMMENDATIONS

Der fliegende Holländer (The Flying Dutchman)

The first in a series of operas that changed the face of opera, *The Flying Dutchman* was first performed in 1843, in Dresden. It's based on a spooky story by Heinrich Heine that follows the adventures of a man doomed to sail the seas until he earns redemption by gaining the love of a virgin and his soul is saved. The music is tempestuous and highly evocative – the Overture has found its way into the standard repertoire of classical symphony orchestras, providing a particularly stunning start to any concert.

Die Meistersinger von Nürnberg (The Mastersingers of Nuremberg)

Another featuring a very famous Overture, this is Wagner's only comic-style opera. As usual, he wrote the libretto himself and the work was first performed in Munich, in 1868. The opera is set in mid-sixteenth century Nuremberg. The essence of the plot lies in the issue of 'true art' being more worthy than 'academic art' – at the time a subject which had a subtle parallel with

Wagner's relationship with the critics. Eduard Hanslick, Vienna's sternest critic of Wagner's work, is portrayed in the opera by the character Beckmesser (Hans Lick in the original version of the libretto!). The subject matter gets a vigorous, uncompromising treatment by Wagner and has been much criticized in certain circles. Nevertheless, it is a fine opera with a strong appeal to an audience who have prior knowledge of its artful references.

Lohengrin

Here again Wagner wrote the libretto for this opera, which was first staged in 1850, in Weimar. The story is based on the medieval Christian legend of the Holy Grail and the historical war between the German King Henry I and the Hungarians. The long and involved plot contains much very fine music including 'The Bridal Chorus', which most people will recognize, even if they have little or no previous knowledge of opera. True to form, Wagner utilizes the forces of a huge orchestra, this time featuring twelve on-stage trumpets in addition to those in the orchestra pit.

Tristan und Isolde

The intricacies of love and sex are the subject matter of this long opera, first performed in Munich, in 1865. It's in three acts and was the first of Wagner's 'music-dramas', as he liked them to be known. There are no big chorus numbers within the opera, instead Wagner employed the method of 'endless melody', whereby the tunes keep on coming. Harmonically *Tristan und Isolde* is one of the most interesting of his works – the chromatic flavour of the music is well suited to the subject and Wagner is at his very best in the famous Prelude and *Liebestod*, which are classic operatic favourites.

Der Ring des Nibelungen (The Nibelung's Ring)
  Das Rheingold (The Rhinegold)
  Die Walküre (The Valkyrie)
  Siegfried
  Götterdämmerung (The Twilight of the Gods)

Completed in 1874, this cycle of four operas was given its first performance in Wagner's own theatre at Bayreuth, the first two in the series having been performed individually in Munich. He described it as 'a theatre festival play for three days and a preliminary evening' and such is the grandiose scale of the work that it precludes an 'overview' here. Suffice it to say that the four sequential operas form the most significant contribution ever made to the medium of opera and that the subjects dealt with include symbolic references to the full range of human emotions (including love and hate, betrayal and broken promises) and behaviour, as well as socialist/Marxist views on the way society was developing at the time.

Parsifal

With his last opera, first performed at Bayreuth, in 1882, Wagner again deals with the Christian legend of the Holy Grail. The character Parsifal, father of Lohengrin, also has a connection with another of Wagner's operas, *Tannhäuser*, in its minstrel Wolfram, who set down this legend in the thirteenth century. Wagner had always wanted to enact Christian ritual on the stage and this 'sacred festival drama' for Easter-time served as a fitting end to his illustrious career.

PUCCINI: *LA BOHÈME* (*Bohemian Life*) and *MADAMA BUTTERFLY*

George Bernard Shaw, a music critic before he became a giant of literature, once said of Puccini that 'he looks more like the heir of Verdi than any of his rivals'. This opinion was widely endorsed and today Puccini is hailed the world over as one of the very finest of operatic composers from any generation. Born on 22 December 1858, in the picturesque Italian town of Lucca, in Tuscany, Giacomo Puccini was one of the fifth generation of Puccinis to be heavily involved in music. The rest were, in the main, church composers, choristers, organists or teachers, but a visit to see Verdi's *Aida* when he was just eighteen years old made such an impression on young Giacomo that he determined opera would be his career. He trained in Milan and was then awarded a place at the Teatro alla Scala – the best result he could have wished for.

Having entered a competition in which his opera entitled *Le Villi* was unsuccessful, he was invited to play the piano and sing at the home of a wealthy art-lover, Marco Sala. Here Puccini performed some extracts of this very opera to a rapturous reception. So impressed were the assembled party-goers, among whom were many influential and important people, that Puccini was immediately signed up by the celebrated publishing house of Giulio Ricordi.

An early disaster with his next opera, *Edgar*, was

followed by the now enormously popular *Manon Lescaut*, the subject of which was altogether more suitable for his gifts: Puccini's music is characterized by wonderful melodies accompanied by dramatic and colourful orchestrations. *Manon Lescaut* was first performed in Turin, on 1 February 1893 and Puccini became a household name overnight. Fame was followed by a certain amount of fortune, which Puccini wisely used to purchase a beautiful home by Lake Massaciuccoli in the little village of Torre del Lago, where he was able to pursue his other love – shooting waterfowl.

He teamed up with librettists Illica and Giacosa for the production of his next three operas, the three that are perhaps his finest and, consequently, his best known: *La Bohème*, *Tosca* and *Madama Butterfly*. The tripartite creative team was not without its problems and there were frequent personality clashes that led to disagreements, but Puccini always had the last word. The two librettists had closely defined roles: Illica would map out the structure of the scenes and develop each episode to the very last detail, while Giacosa would organize the text poetically so that it ran smoothly in verses for the composer to set to music. Puccini had an extraordinary ability to act as the librettists' arbitrator and authoritatively decided upon the way things would turn out. The touch of genius shines through all his work.

Strangely enough, the first performance of *La Bohème* was not at all well received by the critics, who were expecting another lush, romantic work like *Manon Lescaut*. *Tosca*, on the other hand, had quite an impact, being so markedly different in style from the mythological, 'fantastic' offerings of Wagner, who was in full flow at that time. Audiences responded well to the realism and immediacy of Puccini's treatment of playwright Sardou's melodrama, while the first performance of *Madama Butterfly* at La Scala, Milan, was the scene of a fiasco of almost riotous proportions – engineered, it transpired, by Puccini's rivals. The true test of time places these three operas near to the top of most opera lovers' 'all-time-favourites' list and certainly right at the top of the list of most opera singers, who revel in the marvellous roles that Puccini has created for them. The lead sopranos in his operas fare particularly well as Puccini was a master writer of dramatic, impassioned soprano arias. The characterization he gave to these roles was always more powerful than that of the corresponding male leads and it's interesting to note that, of the twelve main operas he wrote, seven are even named after the soprano heroine.

In 1909 the family maid, Doria, committed suicide after enduring a long and painful period of persecution by the composer's wife, who was convinced that Doria was having an affair with Puccini (which she was). This domestic tragedy affected Puccini greatly and his creative talents ceased altogether for some time. He returned to composing with a change of outlook, at first avoiding romantic subjects. His next offering was *La fanciulla del West* (*The Girl of the Golden West*), followed later by *La rondine* (*The Swallow*) and *Il trittico* (*The Triptych*), a three-part opera comprising *Il tabarro*, *Suor Angelica* and *Gianni Schicchi*. None of these met with the widespread acclaim that the earlier operas received and, realizing that they were not his finest material, Puccini set to work on a new opera, the wonderful *Turandot*.

Turandot encompassed the best elements of all that had

gone before – the romantic, lyrical, powerful, and the lighter, comic strands that had so brilliantly been woven together in *La Bohème* some years earlier. Of course, today there is one aria from *Turandot* that almost everyone has heard of: '*Nessun dorma*' ('None shall sleep'). Luciano Pavarotti's recording of this glorious aria was used in Britain as the theme tune for the 1990 World Cup television coverage and subsequently went to the top of the pop charts. This led to the stupendous '*Three Tenors*' concert, screened live from Rome all over the world, and featuring Pavarotti singing alongside Placido Domingo and José Carreras.

Tragically, *Turandot* was not completed by Puccini. He died on 19 November 1924 of throat cancer, in the town of Viareggio. Puccini had made numerous sketches of the music that he intended to use and these were cleverly completed by Franco Alfano. Toscanini conducted the first performance (which was presented exactly as Puccini had left it) at La Scala, Milan, in April 1926. The next evening it was played with the new final scenes by Alfano, which is how it is most often performed today.

SYNOPSIS OF *LA BOHÈME*

Henry Mürger's prose work *Scènes de la Bohème*, written in 1854, was the source of inspiration for this, arguably Puccini's finest opera. The action takes place in the early half of the nineteenth century, as in the original literary work, which was subsequently developed for Puccini's operatic use by the librettists Giuseppe Giacosa and Luigi Illica. The first peformance took place in Turin, in 1896.

Act I opens with Marcello and Rodolfo, two of the 'Bohemians', a painter and poet respectively, trying to keep warm in the dilapidated attic apartment in Paris that they share with two others. It's Christmas Eve and, having no fuel for the stove, they try to think of what they can burn to keep the place at any kind of habitable temperature. A chair is considered, then one of Marcello's paintings, but finally they settle on the manuscript of one of Rodolfo's plays. Colline (a philosopher), one of their flatmates, arrives to see a nice fire blazing, but as the scene draws to a close the fire dies down and a sense of gloom returns.

The fourth and last flat-sharer, Schaunard (a musician), bundles clumsily into the room and to everyone's joy, he is loaded down with food, wine and wood for the fire! To top it all, he has a bag of money, which he throws on the floor. He tells them that the money is part-payment for the music lessons he's been giving a wealthy Englishman. Delighted, the others start to set the table for a celebratory, festive meal. Schaunard insists, however, that they go out for dinner but, while they are enjoying aperitifs before leaving, their land-lord, Benoît, arrives to collect the rent. They purposely embarrass him by teasing him about some young girl that they have recently seen him with and he soon makes his retreat. Marcello, Colline and Schaunard set off for the Café Momus, leaving Rodolfo behind. He says he'll follow in five minutes as he has some writing to finish.

A knock at the door interrupts him and he lets in a pale and flustered girl from the apartment upstairs, Mimì. Her candle has gone out, she explains. She appears to be unwell and, concerned that she might faint, Rodolfo helps her to a chair and relights her candle. A glass of wine soon revives her, but just as she is about to leave she discovers she can't find her door key. Her candle goes out again, as does Rodolfo's, and the two grope around in the darkness. Rodolfo quickly finds the key but hides it even more quickly – he's enjoying this situation and has his mind on other things! Their hands meet and Rodolfo launches into the famous aria '*Che gelida manina*' ('Your tiny hand is frozen'); as they get to know each other a little better, she answers his questions by singing what is probably the finest aria in the opera '*Si, mi chiamano Mimì*' ('Yes, I'm called Mimì') and she tells him how lonely and difficult her life is, scraping a living by embroidering artificial flowers.

Mimì goes on to say that it is really natural flowers that delight her, at which point she is interrupted by the sound of voices from below: Rodolfo's friends are calling from the street. He asks them to keep him a place at the café and the two sing a duet: '*O soave fanciulla*' ('O lovely girl'), aware that they are falling in love. Rodolfo says he will take her to the café for the meal with his friends – and afterwards (he adds), 'who knows what might happen . . .'

The Act closes and the second one opens on the square outside the café, in the Latin Quarter. The scene is a very busy one, with noisy crowds of people, street traders and the like. Rodolfo and Mimì eventually find their way to the others, who are seated at an outside table, and introductions are made. As they place their order for the food, Parpignol the toy-seller bustles by, followed by hordes of children and their mothers. It is a lively and ebullient scene that creates a wonderfully evocative Parisian atmosphere.

Musetta, an old flame of Marcello's, arrives at the café with her new admirer, a rich, older man named Alcindoro. Musetta belittles and angers him by flirting with Marcello in a very provocative way.

At length Musetta finds an excuse to send Alcindoro on an errand and, as soon as he's gone, she falls into a passionate embrace with her former lover, who willingly succumbs! The waiter interrupts the scene by bringing the bill, but, alas, they have all overspent and cannot pay it. The hustle and bustle in the street is accelerated with the marching past of the local band and in the midst of all this commotion the young 'Bohemians' run off without paying. The unfortunate Alcindoro is left to settle up.

Act III is set some two months later at the Barrière d'Enfer, one of the gates of Paris, where we see a typical street scene. Musetta's voice rings out from a nearby building and Mimì, unsure where to search, asks the local sergeant if he knows of a painter living and working nearby. He directs her to the inn, from which the sound of Musetta's voice had been heard earlier. She asks for Marcello, who tells her that he and Musetta have been living there for a month and that they are happy and very busy – he as a painter and Musetta as a music teacher. Mimì asks if Rodolfo is there with them and, on discovering that he is, she's terribly upset and refuses to go in. She bursts into tears and tells Marcello, who's a very sympathetic listener, all about her problems. It appears that she and Rodolfo do love each other but he is an extremely jealous partner. Having heard the whole story,

Marcello consoles her but recommends that they must split up and Mimì reluctantly agrees. All the while they talked, Mimì coughed alarmingly and Marcello has become seriously concerned about her health.

It's early morning and Rodolfo, who has just woken up, appears. Mimì hides and Marcello and Rodolfo have a conversation in which she overhears Rodolfo say that he thinks that he and Mimì should part because she's such a 'coquette'; he goes on to give his real reason, which is that he's worried about her ill health being made worse by the cold, dank conditions of the room they've been sharing – he just isn't able to support her. Mimì can't contain her grief any longer and she bursts into tears. Rodolfo hears her weeping and takes her into his arms. Sadly they agree that they must part and they sing a tender duet, *Donde lieta uscì* ('The place which she left in a happy mood'), while in the background Marcello and Musetta carry on a heated argument.

Act IV opens in the garret-like apartment which Marcello and Rodolfo are sharing, having both broken away from their respective partners. While chatting together it emerges that each has recently seen the other's past lover; both pretend not to care but it is obvious that they do. They can't help but regret that the happy times they spent with the girls are over, but their spirits pick up with the arrival of their old friends Schaunard and Colline bearing loaves and herrings for a meal. Times are hard for these characters and, in order to keep their spirits up, they pretend the modest fare is a marvellous banquet. The party mood intensifies as they dance and Schaunard and Colline hold a mock duel.

Then the door is flung open and Musetta comes in. She

is greatly distressed: Mimì, she says, is extremely ill – she has collapsed in total exhaustion. They make up a bed for Mimì and bring her in. She recovers a little, but it is plain to all that Mimì has not long to live. They have nothing in the larder and the only way they can raise some money to buy Mimì food and drink and to pay for a doctor's visit is by selling some possessions. Musetta takes off her earrings, which she will trade for a muff to warm Mimì's hands and Colline determines to sell his coat. Everyone leaves except Mimì and Rodolfo, who stays by the bedside of his beloved.

The two lovers sing '*Torna al nido la rondine*' ('The swallow returns to its nest') and reminisce about the first time they met. Schaunard, Musetta and Marcello return to find Mimì racked by a consumptive (tubercular) coughing fit. Mimì gratefully accepts the muff from Musetta, but shortly after, slumps back, unconscious. Just as Colline arrives back with the necessary money to pay the doctor who has been called, Schaunard whispers to Marcello that Mimì has died. Rodolfo doesn't know – he thinks she is resting peacefully – but suddenly the dreadful reality dawns on him. Distraught, he throws himself on to the bed and the final curtain falls.

SYNOPSIS OF *MADAMA BUTTERFLY*

First performed some eight years after *La Bohème*, in Milan, *Madama Butterfly* is based on the play by the American writer David Belasco, which was itself based on a story by John Luther Long. Puccini again used the creative team, librettists Giacosa and Illica for this two-act opera. Puccini, on a visit to London in 1900, had seen Belasco's play and been immediately captivated by the idea of using the story as the basis for a new opera. At its first performance the opera was for many reasons a complete flop; it was revised later that same year, this time with the second act divided into two distinct parts and with a number of changes to the names of the characters. The story centres on the relationship and troubles of a US Navy lieutenant, Pinkerton, and his young Japanese wife, Butterfly (Cho-cho-san).

Act I opens with Goro, the marriage broker, showing Pinkerton round the home that the American lieutenant is buying in Japan. Pinkerton is introduced to the servants, one of whom, Suzuki, takes a shine to him. After they have left, Goro waits with Pinkerton for bride-to-be Butterfly to arrive, along with her family and the other guests who will be attending the wedding.

Sharpless, the American Consul, is the first to arrive. Pinkerton takes him round the impressive house and Sharpless praises the rooms, the views of the garden, the harbour and so on. Pinkerton, enjoying every minute of this, expounds his theories about how to achieve happiness in love and marriage and ends by declaring 'America for ever!' as the orchestra plays a snippet of 'The Star-Spangled Banner'.

Butterfly arrives with her friends whereupon, at her instructions, they all fall to their knees at the feet of 'B. F. Pinkerton', as she calls him. Sharpless has a chat with Butterfly and finds out that the girl comes from a good family background, although her father is dead and she is only fifteen years old. In the meantime, Butterfly's relations arrive and the party starts. The servants pass round food and drinks as the guests chatter amongst themselves and, in an aside, Sharpless advises Pinkerton that he should be careful not to upset his bride. After a few minutes, Butterfly requests everyone to bow down low to the two Americans and sheepishly asks Pinkerton if he minds her bringing a few treasured possessions with her. From inside her baggy sleeves she produces a number of items (including a knife sent to her father by the Mikado) and, out of earshot of the assembled crowd, tells Pinkerton that she went the day before to the Mission and became a Christian, so that she would make the perfect wife.

The Imperial Commissioner steps forward with the marriage contract, which he reads aloud before passing it round for the witnesses' signatures. Sharpless repeats his warning to Pinkerton and the Japanese guests drink a toast – 'O Kami! O Kami!' – to the bride and groom. Suddenly Butterfly's uncle, the old Bonze (priest), arrives and immediately confronts Butterfly, demanding to know why she was at the Mission the previous day. He accuses her of abandoning both her religion and her family. The shock is immense and the outraged relatives wish to disown Butterfly. Pinkerton hastily orders them to leave and we hear their irate voices fade away in the distance. Butterfly is comforted by Suzuki, her servant, who shows great concern for her and the Act closes with a beautiful love-duet sung by the 'happy' couple.

Part I of Act II is set some three years later and the opening scene is of Suzuki praying for her mistress, who, apparently is continually weeping. Pinkerton was called away to serve in America shortly after their wedding and Butterfly has not seen him since. In the meantime she has given birth to a son, aptly named Trouble, money is running out and Suzuki has doubts that Pinkerton will ever return. Butterfly, clinging to hope, sings the sublime aria '*Un bel dì*' ('One fine day'), in which she imagines the blissful moment when he will be back in her arms.

Goro, the marriage broker, arrives at the house with the American Consul, Sharpless. Butterfly nervously makes a fuss of them and her incessant chatter prevents either of them from telling her why they have come. She asks them if it is nearly the season for robins to nest in America, as her husband had said he would be returning at that time. She mentions another person that Goro had tried to persuade her to marry – Prince Yamadori, who coincidentally arrives on the scene. Goro, anxious to help Butterfly, remarks to Sharpless that under Japanese law she could divorce Pinkerton for desertion, but Butterfly overhears and reminds him that she has become an American citizen.

Goro leaves them and, now alone with Butterfly, Sharpless reads out the letter from Pinkerton that he has brought. At first she is excited to hear what the letter has to say, but then she becomes distressed on learning that her husband has no plans to return. The scene grows yet more poignant when Butterfly brings her young son Trouble into the room and swears she would rather kill herself than go back to dancing to earn the two of them a living. Sharpless leaves after promising that he will tell Pinkerton about her unhappy circumstances. Suzuki pulls Goro into the room to take issue with him: he has been spreading malicious rumours about Butterfly, suggesting that nobody knows *who* is the real father of Trouble.

Butterfly reacts by drawing a knife on Goro, but then she pushes him away in revulsion.

A cannon announces the arrival of a ship in the harbour. Butterfly and Suzuki can see that the name on its side is *Abraham Lincoln* – Pinkerton's ship! In great excitement, they decorate the house with flowers and Butterfly puts on her wedding gown. Then they make three small holes in the wall-screen so that they and the small boy can peep through to see when Pinkerton is coming. Night falls and Suzuki and Trouble fall asleep, but Butterfly remains awake, watching and waiting.

The second part of Act II opens at daybreak and we hear the voices of the sailors singing down at the harbour. Butterfly is still keeping her vigil at the screen. On awakening, Suzuki, learning that Butterfly has stayed up all night, sends mother and son upstairs to rest, promising to call Butterfly as soon as Pinkerton arrives. No sooner have they left the room than there is a knock at the door and there, at last, is Pinkerton, accompanied by Sharpless. Pinkerton feels so ashamed that he cannot face his wife; he feels even worse when Suzuki asks who the young lady out in the garden is. It is Pinkerton's American wife, Kate. Sharpless tells Suzuki that the new Mrs Pinkerton wishes to adopt Trouble, which news does not meet with a warm reception. Suzuki storms out to talk with Butterfly and a remorseful Pinkerton is put firmly in his place by Sharpless, who is dismayed by Pinkerton's callous conduct.

Pinkerton leaves as Kate comes in to talk to Suzuki. Butterfly arrives to welcome her husband and finds Suzuki in tears next to the American woman. She immediately puts two and two together and Suzuki confirms her worst suspicions. After a moment's thought, Butterfly agrees to hand over her son on one condition: that Pinkerton comes and faces her in half an hour's time. She sends Kate and Sharpless away and Suzuki comforts her, but then she too is sent away as Butterfly says she needs to be on her own.

On taking her father's knife from its case, Butterfly pauses to read the inscription on the blade: '*Con onor muore chi non può serbar vita con onore*' ('He dies with honour who cannot live with honour'). Trouble is pushed into the room by Suzuki, who fears what Butterfly may have resolved to do. Butterfly hugs and kisses her child passionately, gives him an American flag and a little doll to play with and places a blindfold over his eyes. She moves behind the screen and stabs herself with the knife. Pinkerton returns with Sharpless and, as they enter the room, Butterfly staggers out from behind the screen, dramatically points to her son and collapses, dead, on the floor.

Ranking amongst the favourites of most serious opera lovers, Puccini's 'big three' operas *La Bohème*, *Tosca* and *Madama Butterfly* are firmly placed in the standard repertoire of opera companies all over the world. They are really well worth getting to know for not only are the stories captivating and rich with emotion, Puccini's handling of the music is absolutely breathtaking. His lesser-known operas also merit exploration if you become hooked on his style. They include *La fanciulla del west* (*The Girl of the Golden West*), first performed in 1910, and the three-part opera production *Il trittico*, comprising

Il tabarro, *Suor Angelico* and *Gianni Schicchi*, which he first started work on in 1913 and put on the stage some five years later.

FURTHER RECOMMENDATIONS

Manon Lescaut

The work that made Puccini a household name, *Manon Lescaut* was first performed in Turin, in 1893. It is based on the autobiographical novel by the Abbé Prévost, although five authors – Leoncavallo, Marco Praga, Domenico Oliva and last, but by no means least, the famous duo of Illica and Giacosa – collaborated on the libretto. It's wonderful stuff – lush, romantic harmonies, exquisite soprano arias and an engaging story-line.

Tosca

First performed in Rome, in 1900, this is one of Puccini's finest operas. It was produced in collaboration with the librettists Illica and Giacosa and was the first of his works to deal with *verismo*, true realism, sparked off in reaction to the mythological works of Wagner and others.

Turandot

Containing one of the most famous arias from the whole operatic repertoire, '*Nessun dorma*', *Turandot* is an absolute masterpiece. La Scala, Milan, saw the first performance in April 1926 and the story, set in Peking, is elaborate and exciting, combining elements of passion, sex, violence and torture. The score is one of Puccini's greatest, with arguably the most exotic orchestrations he ever conjured.

GERSHWIN: *PORGY AND BESS*

It may seem strange to include in a book about opera a composer who is generally associated with 'shows', 'musicals' and music of the jazz style. However, George Gershwin was one of those rare talents who have the gift for communicating with all kinds of audiences through the medium of music; and, drawing on a story-line that was very dear to his heart, in 1935 he wrote what has become one of the most popular operas ever to have been staged.

George Gershwin came from a rather unsettled background. He was born in 1898, the son of a Russian Jew who was desperately trying to make his way (successfully, as it turned out) in the USA, having emigrated there in the early 1890s. George had a remarkable natural talent and there are several accounts of him, when challenged with a piano at home, being able to play quite complicated tunes within only a few days. This incipient genius manifested itself later when he teamed up with his brother Ira to write numerous popular songs and shows.

He was influenced by composers such as Jerome Kern and Irving Berlin but his own style retained a distinct hallmark, perhaps best exemplified in the all-time favourite *Rhapsody in Blue* – a jazz piano concerto. Right from the first performance of this work, George Gershwin was regarded in all quarters as a composer to be reckoned with. Later compositions included the *Piano Concerto in F* and *An American in Paris*, which also have become popular favourites on the concert platform.

Some ten years later, in 1935, just two years before his tragically early death from a brain tumour, he composed his opera *Porgy and Bess*. Unequivocal about the way he wanted this piece to sound, he specified that a piano should be played on stage and 'in a jazz manner'. All the way through the score there are directions stipulating phraseology and jazz styles to be adopted by both singers and instrumentalists alike.

The story is set in Charleston, South Carolina, among the poor black maritime community of the thirties. The libretto is by Edwin du Bose Heyward and there are additional lyrics contributed by George's brother Ira in collaboration with the librettist. The opera was first performed in New York by an all-black cast of the Theatre Guild.

Synopsis of *Porgy and Bess*

Act I starts with a very atmospheric scene (like one from a movie). It's night-time and fishermen and their families are loafing about outside their homes in Catfish Row. Clara, wife of Jake (one of the fishermen), is singing to her baby that most famous of lullabies, 'Summertime, an' the livin' is easy'. She's having trouble getting her baby off to sleep and Jake tries his hand at the gentle art, but to no avail. Porgy, a beggar and a cripple who can only get about in a little goat-cart, comes along and joins a group of men shooting craps. During the course of the game Porgy reflects on how lonely is the life of a cripple; then suddenly the mood is broken by the arrival of a drunken, burly stevedore, Crown, accompanied by Bess, his woman. Crown buys some dope and starts to pick fights with the assembled gamblers, one of whom, Robbins, suffers a mighty blow and falls to the ground, dead. Crown makes a hasty departure while the drug-pusher, Sporting Life, offers to look after Bess and take her off to New York in search of excitement and a life of crime. Bess refuses, saying she hasn't yet sunk so low and that there's really only one guy she'll feel comfortable with – Porgy.

The next scene is set in a room at the house of the murdered Robbins, whose corpse is lying on the table. Serena, his wife, leads the mourning ceremony, at which she tries to raise some money to pay for the funeral. Bess and Porgy arrive and the kind-hearted Bess offers Serena some money, which at first she refuses, but Bess reassures her that this money did not belong to Crown: it comes from her new love, Porgy. More funds trickle in and then suddenly a policeman and a detective come into the room and arrest Peter, the honey-seller, who, they reckon, will be a sound witness when they finally get their hands on the villain, Crown. The undertaker reluctantly agrees to bury the body for the paltry sum that's been collected, after which the atmosphere changes and the Act closes with Bess leading the crowd in a song of optimism about the good times ahead.

Set one month later, Act II opens at the quayside, where the fishermen are getting ready to go out to sea. Bess is happily installed with Porgy, who leans out of the window of their little dwelling-place and sings the classic 'I got plenty o' nuttin' '. There follows a series of short episodes that together create a highly evocative scene. Sporting Life tries to sell his 'happy dust'; a lawyer arrives offering his services to couples requiring divorces, and an amiable white guy named Archdale calls by, offering to bail out poor old Peter from jail. Sporting Life again attempts to entice Bess away with promises of big pickings in New York, but he is fended off by Porgy. Porgy and Bess are now devoted to each other and they sing the duet 'Bess, you is my woman now'. This tender love-song provides a touching moment of relief prior to the hustle and bustle of the following street scene, where everyone is getting ready for a picnic. Porgy can't go because of his disability, but he insists that Bess should join in and enjoy herself, and he carries on with a reprise of his song 'I got plenty o' nuttin' '.

Over now to the scene of the picnic, which is on Kittiwah Island, where the sleazy drug-pusher sings another hit from this opera, 'It ain't necessarily so' (a song that has since become a 'standard' for musicians from all quarters, particularly in the cabaret field). Drama then ensues as, just as it's time for the boat to leave the island, Crown jumps out on Bess. Furious that she has taken up with the cripple Porgy, he pitches her violently into the bushes.

The scene returns to Catfish Row. A few days have passed and there is further trouble: a hurricane is on its way and Bess has fallen sick. Peter, now released from jail, urges Porgy to get her to the hospital. Above the cries of the vendors in the street, Serena prays for Bess's recovery. Porgy, a tower of strength, reassures her that if Crown ever tries to come and take her away he will protect her. The hurricane breaks and Gershwin's brilliant orchestral music depicts the storm.

At the next switch of scene, everyone at Serena's place is joined together in prayer; they are all terrified of the storm and fearful of the dreadful damage it could inflict. Suddenly Crown bursts into the room. He jeers at their behaviour and makes wild threats, but leaves of his own accord. The praying continues and the Act closes.

A scene of mourning starts Act III. The storm has calmed but one of the fishermen, Jake, who stupidly went out in his boat although he knew that a storm was brewing, has been drowned; and his wife, Clara, who went out to look for him, is also missing. Bess is occupied looking after Clara's baby, when down in the courtyard Crown appears. He's intent on taking Bess back but, just as he walks past Porgy's window, a knife is thrust through – and into his back. Crown falls to the ground, then staggers to his feet, whereupon Porgy grips him around the throat and finishes him off.

Next day, the police arrive and everyone denies knowing who did the evil deed. Porgy is taken off to identify the body and while he's away Bess is harassed again by Sporting Life, who this time successfully plies her with dope. He tells her that now Porgy's gone away, and probably for good; she should be looking forward to a life of plenty with him and that they should sail off to New York on the next available boat. Bess resists his coaxing, but later she takes some more dope . . .

A week passes and Porgy returns. He's won some money shooting craps in jail and has bought presents for

Bess and all his friends. He sings the poignant song, 'Bess, oh where is my Bess?', and they can hardly bring themselves to tell him that she has left. Serena and Maria do their best to comfort him, but Porgy is determined to go to New York in his goat-cart to find Bess. The company unite with him in his bravely optimistic song, 'Oh Lawd, I'm on my way', as the opera closes.

CHAPTER FOUR

Where Next?

The composers and the operas surveyed in the previous chapter are amongst the most popular and distinguished in the development of the entire opera movement. I've tried to achieve a balance between those that are undeniably the most 'important' composers and those who produced good, entertaining and accessible material. Before going any further, however, I must stress that in the whole scheme of things both Carl Maria von Weber and Richard Strauss should probably be included in such a list. These two composers, along with a host of others who must also not be forgotten or dismissed, made significant contributions.

Beethoven, for example, produced one 'classic' opera in *Fidelio* but never wrote another. Similarly Debussy, Offenbach, Leoncavallo, Borodin and Smetana are composers who had 'one-hit wonders' when it came to opera. The 'established critics' may well chide me therefore for including Gershwin with *Porgy and Bess* or, indeed, Bizet and *Carmen* which, it could be argued, fall into this same category. These have been included because of their highly individual and influential style of writing, which led others to follow in their footsteps and to break new ground.

So where exactly do you turn to in your quest for other good operatic material? Most of the famous composers have written operas and during the course of this chapter we'll touch on the best ones to look out for. If you're a fan of Stravinsky's music, for example, it's well worth taking a look at *The Rake's Progress* or *Oedipus Rex*. These won't be everybody's cup of tea, but they contain a lot of marvellous music and are extremely powerful works in their own right. Similarly, if you've heard some of Richard Strauss's 'tone poems', a logical next step would be to give some of his operas a hearing. They possess similar characteristics in their exotic and colourful orchestration, linked with highly emotive subject matters, arresting singing and incredibly dramatic stage treatments.

Here follows, then, a whistle-stop tour of some of the other mainstream composers, beginning with those whose works date from the late Baroque period and ranging through almost three centuries of opera. As a collection it's by no means totally exhaustive, but it includes works by many of the most famous composers, in addition to some you may not have heard of but who also had a distinct 'voice' that should be experienced.

GEORGE FREDERICK HANDEL
(1685–1759)

Handel wrote many operas in the typical Italianate style of the time – adhering to the rules and formats that were firmly laid down. Nevertheless there is a lot to recommend in these operas, particularly if you're keen on Baroque music in general. Suggestions include *Rinaldo* (1711), *Giulio Cesare* (1724), *Orlando* (1733), *Alcina* (1735), *Samson* (1743) and *Serse* (*Xerxes*) (1738), from which his celebrated 'Largo' comes.

LUDWIG VAN BEETHOVEN
(1770–1827)

Beethoven was never terribly inspired to write operas (although, it appears, he yearned to), largely because of the subject matter that other composers were making fashionable at the time. He was not a great one for frivolity and writing in a light-hearted or comic style would have been totally foreign to him. For his one and only opera *Fidelio* he chose the theme of married love and drew various parallels with real-life moral issues. It was first performed in 1805, later revised in 1814 and is quite regularly presented on the operatic stage today, although it's not a box-office 'blockbuster' like, for example, Puccini's *La Bohème*. The overture to *Fidelio* has a unique, almost symphonic, stature of its own and is sometimes used as a concert overture. Beethoven couldn't make up his mind about the start of this opera and previously incorporated the overture that we now know as *Leonora No. 2* in the original score of *Fidelio*, only to alter it in the revised version.

CARL MARIA VON WEBER
(1786–1826)

The German composers who involved themselves in writing operas by and large gained their inspiration from serious literature dealing with 'heavy' romantic subjects or mythological and quasi-supernatural fables. Weber falls into this category and had a huge success on his hands following the first performance of *Der Freischütz* in Berlin, in 1821. *Euryanthe* followed a couple of years later and *Oberon*, his last work, was premiered in 1826. These latter two operas seem to work better as straight pieces of music – there's a plethora of great tunes, beautifully orchestrated in the best German romantic tradition; but the plots are so involved that staging the operas appears to be a formidable challenge for many companies. Wagner, a great admirer, gave the 'graveside eulogy' when Weber's body was returned to Dresden in 1844.

VINCENZO BELLINI
(1801–1835)

Bellini is most often categorized with Rossini and Donizetti as being a brilliant, inspired composer of accessible Italian opera. He was a fine writer of tunes and it is a terrible tragedy that he lived for such a short time. *La Sonnambula* (*The Sleep-Walker*) is a particular favourite, written and first performed in 1831. There are marvellous theatrical devices to be exploited in sleep-walking, the component that gave the opera its name, and Bellini used them all to great dramatic effect.

Throughout his work there are superlative examples of *bel canto* and coloratura soprano writing: in the well-known opera *Norma*, first performed in 1831, the year that Bellini died, '*Casta diva*' ('Chaste Goddess') is not to be missed and the wonderful duet '*Mira, O Norma*' is also a time-honoured favourite.

HECTOR BERLIOZ
(1803–1869)

Most famous for his innovative and exotic *Symphonie Fantastique*, Berlioz composed three operas, none of which has really set the world on fire, although there is some very good music hidden within these scores.

In his first opera *Benvenuto Cellini* (1838), the artist is glorified as a romantic hero, while the subject of *Les troyens* (*The Trojans*) (1858) was firmly based in classical history. *Bèatrice et Bénédict* (1862), on the other hand, is Berlioz's version of Shakespeare's *Much Ado About Nothing* and calls on the singers to recite their lines as well as sing them. Various opera companies around the world occasionally revive all these operas and, again, they are well worth listening to on recordings.

CHARLES FRANÇOIS GOUNOD
(1818–1893)

Gounod was a prolific French composer who, like Berlioz,

wrote three operas, one of which, *Faust*, has remained relatively popular. First performed in Paris, in 1850, and based on the play by Goethe, *Faust* achieved widespread acclaim in its time. It's a big opera, in five acts, that contains some really beautiful music, including the 'Choral Waltz', the 'Soldiers' Chorus' and '*Avant de quitter*' ('Valentin's Farewell'). The 'Jewel Song', too, is a well-worn favourite amongst recorded collections of 'hits from the world of opera'.

Gounod's two other operas, *Mireille* (1864) and *Roméo et Juliette* (1867), have now become obscure rarities due to inconsistencies in the overall quality of the scores.

JACQUES OFFENBACH
(1819–1880)

Offenbach is mainly known for his operettas. He wrote over a hundred and they make for good, lively entertainment. The best known are *Orpheus in the Underworld, La belle Hélène* and *La vie parisienne*. He wrote only one serious, grand scale opera, *Les contes d'Hoffmann* (The Tales of Hoffman), but died before completing it. It is based on the work of the German novelist E. T. A. Hoffmann, who appears as the narrator in this opera. Unusual in its form, having a prologue, three acts and an epilogue, it's full of great music. Ernest Guiraud, who helped complete Bizet's *Carmen*, completed the opera from some of Offenbach's sketches, supplying orchestrations – and recitatives, which are quite often left out these days in order to give the work more direction. It's very enjoyable and much to be recommended.

BEDŘICH SMETANA
(1824–1884)

Along with Dvořák, Smetana was undoubtedly one of the finest Czech composers. He wrote a wealth of superb music encapsulating the spirit of his nation. In 1866 the first performance of what has become the single most popular Czech opera, *The Bartered Bride*, was given in Prague. It's based on an engaging but improbable tale of two young lovers encountering convoluted problems on the road to marriage. The tale ends happily enough and is supported all the way through by the colourful, spirited music, the Overture of which has become a favourite orchestral showpiece in its own right.

ALEXANDER BORODIN
(1833–1887)

One of the members of the celebrated group of Russian composers known as 'The Five', Borodin was taught chemistry and founded a school of medicine for women. He had a great talent for composition and, in a very busy professional life, wrote amongst other works a fine opera, *Prince Igor*. It was, unfortunately, unfinished at his death, but the opera was completed by two of his closest friends, the master musicians Rimsky-Korsakov and Alexander Glazunov. Borodin wrote the libretto himself and the opera was first performed in St Petersburg, in 1890.

Borodin created a fascinating, complex tale, set in the twelfth century, with war and peace the central issues and oriental elements brought in to good effect. It has the same sort of dramatic spectacle as Verdi's *Aida* although the music doesn't have quite the same immediacy about it. Nonetheless, it's lively music and, coupled with such a strong plot, is well worth getting to know if you're a fan of Russian music.

MODEST MUSSORGSKY
(1839–1881)

Mussorgsky was another Russian composer who failed to finish his one and only operatic masterpiece. He was a drunk who lived a disorderly life and died in his early forties. Various composers have since revised or corrected the score to his opera *Boris Godunov*, including his close friend and ally Rimsky-Korsakov, Shostakovich and, more recently, the British conductor and opera scholar David Lloyd-Jones.

Like Borodin, Mussorgsky himself wrote the libretto to this opera based on Pushkin's 24-scene historical play. It's a weighty, serious but thoroughly absorbing piece. One of its most fascinating aspects is the way that Mussorgsky incorporated Russian speech rhythms in the musical language of the opera – a technique which has riveted scholars and musicologists ever since.

PETER ILYICH TCHAIKOVSKY
(1840–1893)

Tchaikovsky wrote eight operas, three of which were based on the writings of the poet Pushkin who also provided the inspiration for Mussorgsky's *Boris Godunov*.

Tchaikovsky is best known as a composer of ballet and orchestral music, although he did write two operas that have remained in the repertoire to this day, even if they are not at the top of most opera lovers' list of favourites. First performed in 1879, *Eugene Onegin* was premiered in Moscow where it was extremely popular and was followed some eleven years later by *The Queen of Spades*, for which Tchaikovsky collaborated on the libretto with his brother.

Of the two, *Eugene Onegin* is the better known and more immediately attractive. It's well written and has more style than *The Queen of Spades*, the usual criticism of which is that the story is a bit far-fetched and the opera rambling in its musical content.

JULES MASSENET
(1842–1912)

Sadly, Massenet's music is often frowned upon by the critics. It's tuneful and harmonic and has been criticized for being too sweet and romantically overstated. Nevertheless, such music holds great appeal for huge numbers of people and one of his tunes, the 'Meditation' from *Thaïs*, is so incredibly popular that it seems churlish to give the composer anything but the highest praise for having written this. Massenet wrote two operas that are worthy of our attention here: *Manon*, which is based on a story focusing on sex and religion and which was first performed in 1884; and, later, *Werther* (1893), which is based on the writings of Goethe and is altogether a more serious work. Both of them made quite an impact and remain engaging works for present-day audiences.

ENGELBERT HUMPERDINCK
(1854–1921)

A student and assistant of Richard Wagner's at Bayreuth, the little known (but famous in name) composer Engelbert Humperdinck was a real opera *aficionado*. He wrote six operas, of which we need only concern ourselves here with his most famous – *Hänsel und Gretel*. First performed in Weimar, in 1893, it is an unusual work in that it sports an almost entirely female cast and by the very nature of its subject matter, (a 'doctored' fairy tale by the Brothers Grimm) is designed to appeal to children – which it does with considerable success. *Hänsel und Gretel* is a lovely work and although some may criticize it for being simple in its construction and musical language, it is full of subtlety and charm.

LEOŠ JANÁČEK
(1854–1928)

Many classical music enthusiasts will be familiar with Janáček's masterpiece, the *Sinfonietta*, an orchestral showpiece of great quality. Janáček was also extremely talented at composing for the voice: he wrote half a dozen operas, the most famous of which are *Jenufa* (1904), *Katya Kabanova* (1921), *The Cunning Little Vixen* (1924) and *From the House of the Dead* (first performed in 1930). This is fascinating music that is very much in the Czech idiom. For this reason, these operas do not translate at all well into other languages and part of their inherent beauty is in the way the language is interpolated with the music.

All the works mentioned here are given fairly regular airings by opera companies throughout Europe.

RUGGIERO LEONCAVALLO
(1858–1919)

Not the best known of composers, the Italian Leoncavallo wrote one of a pair of operas that are now frequently performed in the same programme at opera houses all around the world. '*Cav* and *Pag*', as they are affectionately known amongst British opera lovers, are *Cavalleria rusticana* by Mascagni and *Pagliacci* by Leoncavallo. *Pagliacci* is his only well-known piece of music but it's wonderful and should not be overlooked. It includes the memorable '*Vesti la giubba*' ('On with the motley'), which is a firm favourite amongst all opera lovers. Leoncavallo uses the technique of depicting a play within a play very effectively and a wealth of good tunes, beautifully orchestrated, make this a real gem.

CLAUDE DEBUSSY
(1862–1918)

The 'Father of the Impressionist School', Debussy is unquestionably one of the most gifted of the late-nineteenth-century composers. His haunting, shimmering piano pieces are matched by his lush orchestral works like *La Mer* and the *Nocturnes*. First performed in Paris, in 1902, Debussy's only five-act opera *Pelléas et Mélisande* is based on a play by Maurice Maeterlinck. It's a tragic drama in which Debussy's remarkable use of the orchestra is equalled by his stunning writing for the voices. Always subtle in its expression, this is music of great intensity and parallells have been drawn between this opera and excerpts of Mussorgsky's *Boris Godunov* which Debussy had heard and enjoyed some years before. Maeterlinck and Debussy fell out before the first performance of *Pelléas et Mélisande* as Maeterlinck was deeply upset that his wife wasn't chosen for the title role.

PIETRO MASCAGNI
(1863–1945)

Another one-hit wonder composer, Mascagni wrote fifteen operas in all, but his first, *Cavalleria rusticana* ('Rustic Chivalry') is his only famous piece. It was first performed in Rome, in 1890, and is set in a Sicilian village at Easter-time, which provides the essence of the story – village life, the Mafia and the interactions of the community members. So all the usual thematic strands of love, hate, revenge and religion are woven together to form a delightful operatic cameo.

RICHARD STRAUSS
(1864–1949)

The German composer Richard Strauss was one of the most distinguished contributors to the world of opera in the twentieth century. In some ways his work bears a certain similarity to that of Richard Wagner, in that Strauss also used recurring thematic devices and his subject matters were serious, passionate and shocking; but he managed to contain his work in a way that Wagner would never have wished to, with the result that Strauss's operas are more compact and the action moves at a much faster pace.

Salome was based on a play by Oscar Wilde and was first performed in Dresden, in 1905. It depicts a tale in which Herod, infatuated with Salome, promises her anything she desires if she will perform the Dance of the Seven Veils for him. This she carries out and claims the head of John the Baptist in return. Herod at first refuses but eventually, after some intrigue and diversion in the action, John the Baptist's head is duly served up and Salome lasciviously kisses its lips. So appalled is Herod by this, he orders that Salome be crushed to death beneath his soldiers' shields. Fantastic, strong stuff, this one-act opera is probably the most powerful I have ever experienced.

His opera *Elektra* came four years later. It is based on some of the writings of Sophocles and, again, it is powerful and dramatic from start to finish, incorporating corruption, decadence and terror within the historic setting of ancient Mycenae. *Der Rosenkavalier* was first staged in 1911, in Dresden and is among the finest works that Richard Strauss composed. It retains much of the comic element of the libretto (written by Hugo von Hofmannsthal); one of the lead characters, a boy whose voice has not yet broken, is played by a female singer, and is called upon to dress up as a girl (shades of Mozart here!). This charade is developed to the point where we have love scenes in which no males are present. The unfolding of the tale is brilliantly handled by Strauss, whose orchestral writing is second to none in this work. He wrote many other operas, among the best of them, *Ariadne auf Naxos*, *Daphne* and *Capriccio*, which are also worth investigating if you are, or become, a Strauss addict.

IGOR STRAVINSKY

(1882–1971)

The genius of the Russian composer Stravinsky is evident in his extraordinary ballet scores for *The Rite of Spring*, *Petrushka* and *The Firebird*, to name but a few. He brought his unique approach to the world of opera in a number of works, of which the most significant is *The Rake's Progress*. Before this work, however, he had written one or two 'operas' of lesser standing, including *Solovey* (The Nightingale) and a variety of pieces that crossed over the boundaries of solely instrumental into song, dance and speech and which don't quite fall into the specific category of opera. *L'histoire du soldat* (The Soldier's Tale) a piece that has remained popular to this day, is a case in point. In it actors narrate a lengthy text to a suite of music played by a small instrumental ensemble and the action is supplemented by the inclusion of a ballet dancer halfway through the proceedings – both of which features contribute enormously to this impressive and dramatic work. *Oedipus Rex* is more like a cross between an opera and an oratorio and is inspired by the work of Sophocles; curiously, the libretto was written by the celebrated Jean Cocteau and subsequently translated into Latin at the wish of the composer. Again, Stravinsky employs the services of a narrator to tell the story in the native language of the audience.

The Rake's Progress is the perfect example of opera from Stravinsky's 'neo-classical period'. It has traditional recitatives and arias and the flavour of music from the eighteenth century, though with unexpected notes. It's unmistakably 'Stravinsky' and has an intensity that presents a unique sound to our ears. A series of engravings by Hogarth provided the original inspiration for the work and W. H. Auden and Chester Kallman were brought in to write the English libretto. The first performance was given in Venice, in September 1951.

ALBAN BERG
(1885–1935)

From the 'Second Viennese School', Alban Berg was one of the disciples of the founder of that school, Arnold Schoenberg. Schoenberg himself wrote four operas, none of which hold great interest for opera lovers these days. However, his protégé Berg has provided two notable offerings to the medium, both of which are regularly performed and both of which have become significantly influential.

Based on the play *Woyzeck* by the German writer Georg Büchner, Berg's opera *Wozzeck* was first performed in Berlin, in 1925. Wozzeck is a soldier and the opera follows the disturbing tale of his life from the time he had fathered a child out of wedlock, through to the dramatic moments when he murders the mother of the child and then commits suicide. Musically the opera is extremely powerful, although unless one is familiar with atonal music (that is, music that is not written in any particular key and that has no significant 'tonal' relationships of any sort) it sounds very strange indeed. *Lulu*, on the other hand (first performed in its incomplete version in 1937 and performed 'complete' in 1979), uses the musical language known as 'serial technique' – which is to say the twelve tones of the scale are employed in highly ordered and mathematical configurations. This principle of order and configuration is also applied to all the other aspects of phraseology, dynamics and structure of the music, giving the piece a cool sort of starkness that many find unapproachable. The opera deals with various aspects of 'womanhood' – beauty, sexuality, infidelity and, finally, prostitution – painting an extraordinary picture that Berg handles brilliantly. If the sound, or the very idea, of serialistic music doesn't immediately put up barriers for you, then this opera comes highly recommended.

SERGEI PROKOFIEV
(1891–1953)

Known as a great all-round composer, Prokofiev wrote seven operas, only a few of which get performed with any regularity. A couple are well worth knowing as they are brilliantly constructed and contain some very fine music: *The Love for Three Oranges* and *The Fiery Angel*, being particular favourites. Employing an extremely large cast, the grand opera *War and Peace*, first performed in Leningrad, in 1946, is based on Tolstoy's epic novel of the same name. It's a vast work consisting of a large number of continuous scenes, though it is occasionally presented in a cut-down version.

KURT WEILL

(1900–1950)

Kurt Weill collaborated with the Marxist dramatist Bertolt Brecht to produce *Die Dreigroschenoper* (The Threepenny Opera). A cross between a musical and an opera, it embodies this German composer's inimitable style and has a wide appeal. Weill had the gift of writing music that was immediately accessible on first hearing – like many modern musicals and unlike many modern operas. His subject matters were always fascinating; in *The Threepenny Opera* the story revolves round a collection of beggars, thieves, highwaymen and prostitutes, and culminates in a thought-provoking moral message to society.

MICHAEL TIPPETT

(born 1905)

The English composer Sir Michael Tippett has used the medium of opera to convey to his listeners many of his deepest feelings about man and society. His first opera, *The Midsummer Marriage* (1955), deals with mystical ritual and two couples seeking the true meaning of love and marriage. Tippett has himself drawn the obvious parallels with Mozart's *Die Zauberflöte* (*The Magic Flute*). His handling of the opera is remarkable in its achievement and while this is quite definitely 'modern music' to our ears, it has moments of extraordinary beauty and eloquence.

Equally profound and fascinating subjects are

addressed in his other operas, among the best are *King Priam* (1962), *The Knot Garden* (1970), *The Ice Break* (1977) and *New Year* (1980).

DMITRI SHOSTAKOVICH
(1906–1975)

After the satirical opera *The Nose* (1930), Shostakovich wrote one further opera, entitled *Lady Macbeth of the Mtsensk District*. It was first performed in Leningrad and then, two days later, in Moscow as *Katerina Izmailova*, the title it has retained to this day. It was very well received in the first few years and was performed many times both in Russia and throughout Europe. However, a critic from the national newspaper *Pravda*, denounced it as 'chaos in place of music' and, as with much of his music, Shostakovich was forced to revise the manuscript to make it acceptable to the authorities – which it did eventually become, although not until 1963, some ten years after Stalin's death.

The opera is based on a story by Nikolai Leskov in which a bored housewife, Katerina, poisons her father-in-law and helps her lover, Sergey, to strangle her husband. When the murder is discovered (on their wedding day), they are captured by the authorities and sent away to exile in a Siberian prison-camp. Here, Sergey, tiring of Katerina, has an affair with another prisoner and Katerina drowns her before she herself commits suicide in the same fashion. It's quite a tale – not all doom and gloom as this brief synopsis might suggest, as Shostakovich's extraordinary ability to bring irony and wit into the music provides the vital lighter moments in this fascinating work.

BENJAMIN BRITTEN
(1913–1976)

One of the most respected twentieth-century British composers, Benjamin Britten made a significant contribution to the world of opera. This started in 1945 with his highly acclaimed *Peter Grimes*. Set in the small fishing town 'the Borough' (recognizable as Aldeburgh, in Suffolk, where Britten lived) on the east coast of England in the 1830s, the opera focuses on the immoral and cruel antics of the main character, the gay fisherman Peter Grimes, within the community. Unusually, the opera has no overture and also contains a series of orchestral interludes that play an important musical role in the structure of the whole.

In 1951 he wrote another full-scale opera, *Billy Budd*, featuring an all-male cast and set at sea on board a ship, while his later compositions in the operatic style all take the form of chamber operas – employing smaller instrumental forces. Amongst these, four stand out as being gems in the repertoire: *The Rape of Lucretia* (1946), *Albert Herring* (1947), *The Turn of the Screw* (1954) and *A Midsummer Night's Dream* (1960). Of these, my particular favourite is *The Turn of the Screw*, based on the ghost story by Henry James and given its first performance in Venice, in 1954. It's a very powerful piece of drama in its own right and Britten's haunting music makes an equally impressive impact when this is produced and directed well.

★   ★   ★

Amongst other living composers who have written operas there are several who deserve special mention here. No-one will disagree, I think, that their music appeals strongly to only a relatively small sector of the classical music world, but nevertheless they have made bold statements in their music and are paving the way for new generations of writers. Sir Peter Maxwell Davies has made two significant contributions: *Taverner* (1972) and *The Lighthouse* (1980). Sir Harrison Birtwistle's *Punch and Judy* is also something of a classic (though at the first performance Benjamin Britten walked out because he thought it too violent and inappropriate in its treatment) and he's followed this up with *The Mask of Orpheus* and, most recently, *Gawain*, a heavy but immensely powerful work.

The American composers Philip Glass and John Adams have made an impact with several of their latest works. Glass's *Akhnaten* was brilliantly presented by the English National Opera in London and he formerly made an impression in Paris with *Einstein on the Beach*; John Adams scored a big hit with *Nixon in China*, first performed in Houston and then brought to the Edinburgh Festival in the late eighties. Carlisle Floyd has also achieved quite a following and considerable recognition in the USA with two operas, namely *Wuthering Heights* and *Susannah*, and one mustn't forget the late Leonard Bernstein, whose *West Side Story* has become a timeless classic, appealing to music lovers of all persuasions.

CHAPTER FIVE

Profiles of the Stars

There are a number of virtuoso talents from the world of opera who have become household names and we are now going to look in some detail at their backgrounds, the way that they have risen to fame and how they have achieved cult status. There are also many fine singers who are equally gifted but who have not won such rapturous acclaim from the media. We will consider some of these as well.

On 7 July 1990 three outstanding artists performed together in a concert staged at the Baths of Caracalla, Rome. The *Three Tenors* concert featured Luciano Pavarotti, Placido Domingo and José Carreras singing alongside a 240-strong line-up of musicians and was conducted by Maestro Zubin Mehta. The event was televised and transmitted to the largest audience that the world has ever seen for a concert of classical music. It was a spectacle that captured the rapt attention of both the public and the media and the recording made that night is also one of the most successful of all time. This phenomenon poses the question: is the public just hungry for more spectacular events like the *Three Tenors Live From Rome* or is it genuinely hooked on classical music, avidly visiting the opera and buying boxed sets of CDs featuring their favourite singers? Promoters and record companies alike are trying to support both possibilities. There are opera gala nights at the main concert halls in capital cities and 'spectacular performances' at huge major venues in Europe and Japan while, at the same time, record companies have been swift to release collections of the most popular pieces from opera in every guise imaginable.

What is needed – and what this book sets out to provide – is a convenient guide not only to the best operatic works and individual pieces but also to the leading performers. We are fortunate to be living in an age when there is a wealth of fine artists presenting this music and a handful of supreme talents who have opened up the world of opera for us all.

We begin with profiles of the four artists who have achieved the unique distinction of appealing not only to those already captivated by a love of opera but also to those who never gave opera a second thought until a few years ago. There then follow short descriptions of a number of the other significant opera performers of today, up-and-coming stars and some of the great names of the past.

LUCIANO PAVAROTTI

Perhaps the best known singer in the world, Luciano Pavarotti has demonstrated more than anyone else that opera can be enjoyed by everyone. Following his huge hit at the Italia '90 celebrations he wowed a similar kind of audience with his artistry at the infamous 'wash-out' concert in London's Hyde Park in 1991. Undoubtedly one of the finest tenors there has ever been, he is also held in the very highest respect in the more formal opera circuit where he performs the lead tenor roles at all the major opera houses around the world.

Pavarotti made his début in 1961 at Reggio Emilia in Puccini's *La Bohème*. The occasion was a triumph and he was subsequently invited to sing at opera houses throughout Italy. Two years later offers were flooding in from all over Europe and his début at London's Covent Garden (where he stood in at the very last minute for di Stefano, who was indisposed) met with the highest praise; he was immediately invited back and the event marked the start of countless appearances in the ensuing years. His repertoire encompasses all the great tenor parts but he's perhaps most renowned for his Italianate romantic hero roles by Donizetti, Rossini, Puccini and Verdi. Among my particular favourites are his renditions of the Duke in Verdi's *Rigoletto* and Rodolfo in Puccini's *La Bohème*.

His recordings have also sold more copies than those of any other operatic artist and most recently we have seen the two *Essential Pavarotti* discs storming their way to the top of the charts. His whole catalogue of recordings can be given the very highest recommendation, especially the works mentioned above and the one in which he plays the role he holds dearest to his heart – that of Nemorino in Donizetti's *L'elisir d'amore*.

On a more personal level, it's interesting to note that in order to keep his voice in great shape Pavarotti has very special requirements when he's out on the road touring the world. His entourage are under strict instructions to ensure his well-being and comfort. His diet is naturally of particular importance, as is the décor and condition of his hotels. There must be no wet paint and no recent decorating: such hazards can greatly affect the voice, as can the effects of highly pollinated flowers, which are banned in the near vicinity of Maestro Pavarotti. Don't think that these are the whims of an overly sensitive and 'precious' artist. They are essential requirements for a man who has been given one of God's most outstanding musical gifts. An exceptionally large man, Pavarotti's size has taken its toll on his health; he has problems with his hips and knees and is frequently driven around in a kind of golfers' buggy to avoid undue stress on the failing limbs. Opera singers are often portrayed in caricatures as overweight and perspiring copiously from the efforts of singing. However, there definitely is a positive factor in having a large frame when it comes to operatic singing and one only has to look at other artists like Joan Sutherland to realize that this is true. Pavarotti experienced an embarrassing incident linked to this very subject. A few years ago, when performing in Puccini's *Tosca* at the Paris Opera, he was lying stretched out on a chair, with Tosca perching elegantly on top, when the inevitable happened . . . the chair collapsed spectacularly under the strain, leaving the two artists flailing about on the stage floor. There was unrestrained mirth from the audience. Certainly a night to remember – or one to forget in the case of Maestro Pavarotti.

Skipping lightly over this unfortunate mishap, let me press home that if ever you have the chance to hear this man in the flesh, seize the opportunity. Pavarotti is, without doubt, a living legend.

PLACIDO DOMINGO

A totally all-round musician, Placido Domingo is not only one of *the* most celebrated lyric-dramatic tenors but also an outstanding pianist and conductor. It is, of course, as a singer that he is best known and he has appeared at all the world's most illustrious opera houses and on record-ings with such conducting stars as Claudio Abbado, Carlo Maria Giulini, Zubin Mehta, Daniel Barenboim and the late Herbert von Karajan.

He was born in Madrid in 1941 and taken to Mexico by his family when he was just nine years old. He came from a highly musical family – both his parents were quite well-known zarzuela singers (zarzuela is a form of Spanish operetta) – and so it came as no surprise that he showed a keen interest and, later, a considerable talent when it came to music – singing in particular. After a period of formal training at the Mexico City Conservatory he quickly became very successful and well-known, with offers of engagements flooding in from all over the world. Having initially landed a part in the show *My Fair Lady*, he quickly moved on to bigger and better things and subsequently made spectacular débuts in operas at Dallas and the Metropolitan in New York.

Since those early days at the beginning of the sixties,

Domingo has also appeared throughout Europe. Unlike Pavarotti and Carreras, in addition to being totally at home with the famous Italian roles he has made a significant impression with works in the German language, such as Weber's *Oberon* and Wagner's *Die Meistersinger* and *Tannhäuser*.

Showing considerable flair in the commercial field too, Domingo has even released a moderately successful pop single with Jennifer Rush and, like Pavarotti, has also given a concert in a park – New York's Central Park – the only classical artist ever to have done so. He also has a passion for singing *canzoni* (traditional Spanish songs), *chansons*, popular hits and songs from operettas; he is quoted as saying that he hopes if people have heard him singing this kind of music and their curiosity then leads them to listening to him in an operatic role, the world of opera will truly be opened up – 'If I really consider the matter carefully, that is probably the most important aspect for me'.

Placido Domingo has made in excess of 170 recordings. Among my personal recommendations are *Essential Domingo*, for gaining an overview of the man's enormous talent, and then Verdi's *Aida* recorded with Claudio Abbado, which also features the soprano Katia Ricciarelli and the Orchestra of La Scala, Milan. For a more light-hearted listen and to appreciate his extraordinary versatility, try *Be My Love* or *Domingo Sings Tangos*. He has also appeared in numerous video versions of operas, and his good looks and remarkable talent are perfect for TV.

Talking of versatility, there's a famous story about Domingo in this regard. His PR agent suggested the idea of filming him conducting an orchestra in famous tenor arias and then running the movie at Carnegie Hall with the great man himself singing live to the film – *Domingo Conducts Domingo*. It seemed a brilliant plan, a marketing man's dream, until Domingo pointed out, apparently in all seriousness: 'But if I make a mess of the concert, I won't be able to blame the conductor!' Even if this remark was made in jest, it certainly contains an element of truth for many performers, who do like to have someone to blame if things don't go according to plan. Be that as it may, for Domingo such a contingency rarely arises: he is without doubt one of the finest artists of our time.

JOSÉ CARRERAS

Also of Spanish origin, José Carreras was born in Barcelona in 1946 and was quickly hailed as a child prodigy. He had a phenomenal voice as a youngster and it has developed into one of the most beautiful and engaging of tenor voices the world has ever heard.

By the age of eleven Carreras was already appearing at the Teatro Liceu in Madrid, taking the role of the boy in Manuel de Falla's *Master Puppet Show*, and from that time he never looked back. He was talent-spotted very early on by one of the world's most celebrated sopranos, Montserrat Caballé, and it was she who gave him enormous encouragement and assistance in his first years in the profession. The two appeared together on stage on numerous occasions and made quite a formidable duo.

Carreras has an extraordinarily large repertoire which includes some sixty operas. He is also noted for his superb artistry on the recital stage and has received immense acclaim at his concerts in London, New York, Vienna, Salzburg, Berlin, Munich, Tokyo, Barcelona, Madrid and Rome. He's made over forty recordings of operas and twenty recital and anthology compilations – no mean feat for a man who has not yet reached the age of fifty.

Familiar to a wider audience through his involvement in Leonard Bernstein's concert-style recording of *West Side Story*, José Carreras has made a point of refusing to be limited in his choice of repertoire. The televised recording sessions for *West Side Story* may well have opened the public's eyes to the extreme pressures soloists have to endure when working alongside prima donnas, highly-strung musicians and so on. Carreras dealt admirably with the problems of coping with Bernstein's demanding standards, but it was fascinating to see the tensions between the two artists simmering in front of the cameras.

In 1987, three years before his triumph on the stage of the *Three Tenors Live From Rome* concert (the idea for which is reported to have been his own), the world was shattered to hear the news that José Carreras was suffering from leukaemia. Having undergone punishing medical treatment, he emerged from the trauma and climbed back on to the concert platform just over a year later, when he sang to an audience of 150,000 that included the Queen of Spain. Since that time Carreras has been dedicated to raising funds for leukaemia research and has also set up a special international foundation to fight the disease.

I recommend you to listen to any of his compilation anthologies or his wonderful recording with Ricciarelli of Puccini's *Tosca*, conducted by Herbert von Karajan.

DAME KIRI TE KANAWA

Between 600 and 700 million people are estimated to have watched Dame Kiri Te Kanawa singing Handel's *Let The Bright Seraphim* at the Royal Wedding of Prince Charles and Lady Diana Spencer in the summer of 1981. She was of course already held in the highest esteem throughout the music world, but this historic event made her a household name overnight. Her voice has consistently won the praise of audiences and critics alike. It has a unique purity of tone which, coupled with her extraordinary musical perception and sense of phrasing, results in Dame Kiri Te Kanawa standing out as one of the most gifted musical icons of our generation.

Dame Kiri was born in New Zealand and, following her initial period of study there, was the recipient of numerous prizes and awards for outstanding musical achievement. She came to the operatic stage remarkably early, after a further period of study, this time at the London Opera School. She was still in her early twenties when she had the call to sing at London's Covent Garden, as the Flower Maiden in Wagner's *Parsifal*. So stunning was her performance that the legendary conductor Sir Colin Davis immediately invited her to take the part of the countess in Mozart's *Marriage of Figaro*. The rest is history – she quickly became internationally renowned and has performed all over the world singing the widest cross-section of repertoire imaginable.

Particularly noted for her Mozart, Puccini and Verdi roles, Dame Kiri is splendid, too, appearing in the works of both Richard and Johann Strauss and also when performing Spanish, French and German songs in recital,

She has made her mark with great aplomb on the concert platform, notably in works such as Mahler's *Fourth Symphony*, *The Four Last Songs* by Richard Strauss, in Handel's *Messiah* and the Brahms *German Requiem*.

As a cross-over artist she is also unrivalled in her achievements, having appeared on the Bernstein *West Side Story* recording, Decca's *My Fair Lady* and a delightful album entitled *Blue Skies* where she is joined by Nelson Riddle in a collection of popular American songs. Recently Dame Kiri became involved too in the album of music dedicated to the Rugby World Cup finals of 1991, singing an adapted version of a piece by Gustav Holst under the new title, *World in Union*. For many this recording was a very welcome release providing an anthem-like song that is a rousing and an ethically sound piece of work; for others it was a distasteful, bastardized version of a timeless classic.

Dame Kiri's revelation on a TV chat show that she would love to have been Tina Turner strutting her stuff in a pop arena, gives one a hint of the latent show-biz charisma that has until now been hiding behind the most beautiful, refined exterior in the world of classical music. She also has a fine reputation as a golfer and in 1982 was made a Dame Commander of the British Empire for her services to music.

CHAPTER SIX

Who To Look Out For –
Singers and Directors

If you're about to go and choose an operatic recording or you are hoping to pay a visit to the opera, whose names should you be looking out for? The cast lists on the CDs are quite bewildering unless you know who is best suited to which roles, so, in an effort to assist you in this process, this chapter gives brief details of some of the singers and directors. We begin with the singers. What follows is not a comprehensive list of *everyone* who has been recorded or who is currently performing on stage, and for obvious reasons I've focused mainly on the great recording artists, but it does include a good cross-section of singers from the past and the present who have undoubtedly made their mark.

At the end of the chapter are brief résumés of a handful of directors who have made a significant impact on the world of opera by their contributions to the staging of these great works.

(Entries in the two lists that follow are in alphabetical order.)

THE SINGERS

Thomas Allen, born in 1944, is one of Britain's most celebrated baritones. As well as having a beautifully refined voice, which he uses to excellent dramatic effect, he's a great actor. I find him at his best in the roles of Mozart's operas, (he's among the most popular Don Giovannis), but he is a fine all-rounder.

June Anderson is an American soprano who has found fame and fortune particularly in performing roles from the great Bellini and Donizetti operas. She has a marvellous large voice that is also remarkably agile, which makes her eminently suitable for a great variety of roles.

Dame Janet Baker is one of Britain's most illustrious mezzo-sopranos and has long been recognized for her impeccable sense of musicianship. She was created a Dame Commander of the Order of the British Empire in 1976 and is now firmly established as the *grande dame* of British singing. Always a singer of great intensity, she has made some of the finest recordings of early works by Gluck, Handel and Mozart as well as some highly memorable ones of the music of Benjamin Britten.

Agnes Baltsa is a mezzo-soprano who was born in

Greece in 1944. She made her sensational début at Frankfurt in 1968 in the role of Cherubino from Mozart's *Marriage of Figaro* and creates a sense of excitement that never fails to grip the attention of her audience. A fine actress, her voice is strikingly clear and agile and she is perhaps at her best in the coloratura works of Bellini, Donizetti and Rossini, although she has also made her mark in Bizet's *Carmen*.

Cecilia Bartoli was 'discovered' by the Italian TV-mogul Peppo Baudo, husband of the wonderful soprano Katia Ricciarelli. Bartoli is arguably one of the most glamorous singers on the current opera circuit and her beauty is matched by her superb artistry as a mezzo-soprano. Although still only in her mid-twenties she has already achieved considerable standing throughout the world with a big recording contract for Decca and a string of engagements spanning the next five years. She is particularly suited to the works of Rossini and Mozart, which are among the first recordings she has made; of special mention is the marvellous *Rossini Heroines* recorded with the Orchestra of the Teatro la Fenice, conducted by Ion Marin.

Kathleen Battle possesses one of the most exquisite light, agile soprano voices that I have ever heard. A most beautiful woman too, she is in great demand at all of the major opera houses and is renowned for her prima-donna temperament. It is said that for a recent one-stop engagement in Denmark she had to move hotel three times before being totally satisfied with her surroundings – and the last room was only acceptable once the colour of the walls had been changed. She commands extremely high fees and, temperamental or not, is worth every penny. Listen to her exquisite voice on her recording of Donizetti's *L'elisir d'amore* with Luciano Pavarotti, or, one in the non-operatic mould, the solo part in Mahler's *Fourth Symphony*.

Teresa Berganza is a Spanish mezzo-soprano who has consistently performed at the very highest level in everything that she has done. In the late sixties and early seventies there were few to match her in the standard repertoire. She is particularly noted for her portrayal of Rosina in Rossini's *Barber of Seville* and for Cinderella in the opera of the same name.

Carlo Bergonzi is renowned as one of the fine 'old-school' romantic tenors. His voice is highly individual and he was marvellous in all the great Verdi tenor roles, particularly as the Duke in *Rigoletto* and as Radames in *Aida*.

Jussi Björling is one of my favourite tenors. He lived only until the age of forty-nine but in a short lifetime made some of the very finest recordings, including a memorable one of Puccini's *La Bohème* alongside soprano Victoria De Los Angeles, with Sir Thomas Beecham conducting.

Grace Bumbry has had an unusual and unsettled career as a contralto and a soprano. She is a fine actress and has an arresting voice, but she has undertaken a number of roles that were not quite suited to her range – and this, in many people's view, has not helped her overall development in the world of opera.

Montserrat Caballé has had a long and memorable career, although at times her performances have been criticized for being somewhat erratic. In her prime her voice was the very model of perfection and she excels in all the *bel canto* repertoire. Her voice is absolutely sublime and she has the ability to sing with an extraordinary sense of phrasing. She was one of the first operatic artists to become involved in the now-popular 'cross-over' market by recording a song entitled *Barcelona* with the late Freddie Mercury of the pop group Queen.

Maria Callas is the Marilyn Monroe figure of opera. To encapsulate her life and work in a few short sentences is wellnigh impossible; suffice it to say that, in my humble opinion, she was the finest-ever soprano and many of her performances captured on record are beyond compare. Her ability as an actress was also held in the highest regard. Listen to her in Puccini's *Tosca* or in Bellini's *Norma* for staggering examples of her art. Here was a true genius who was renowned for, amongst other things, walking out of performances, becoming grossly overweight at one time (fifteen stone!) – having previously had a 'model-figure' – for having affairs with high-society men, including the Greek shipping tycoon Aristotle Onassis, and for an untimely, lonely and tragic death in 1977 aged fifty-three.

Enrico Caruso has been the inspiration for many of today's finest tenors. One of the first artists in the history of recorded music, he has become a legend both for his artistic contribution and for the fact that others were so encouraged to hear what spectacular results could be achieved they too went to studios and made recordings. There are many recordings of all his greatest performances currently available (including ones on CD, thanks to the advancement in restorative technology). An absolutely superb musician, he had a magnificent voice that at times could be lyrical, heroic, dramatic and exhilarating: he was in many people's opinion the finest tenor ever.

Ileana Cotrubas was born in Romania and is one of the few sopranos of international repute to have hailed from that country. She is noted largely for her acting abilities and on the strength of these alone she could undoubtedly have carved a highly successful career. The extraordinary intensity of character portrayal in her voice, although at times uneven in quality, has featured in many fine recordings of the Mozart operas, as Violetta in Verdi's *La traviata* and as Tatyana in Tchaikovsky's *Eugene Onegin*.

Victoria De Los Angeles was one of the most beautiful of sopranos ever to grace the world's opera stages. Of Spanish origin, she was naturally wonderful in Bizet's *Carmen* and her purity of voice was also well suited to all the Puccini roles, her Mimi from *La Bohème* being particularly highly praised.

Brigitte Fassbaender is one of the great mezzo-sopranos to hail from Germany (she was born in Berlin in 1939). She has an exciting, dramatic voice that is well suited to roles in works by Richard Strauss and Mozart and is very well known too for her performances on the concert platform as a recitalist and a singer of *lieder*. Also a producer and gifted teacher, Fassbaender has many devoted pupils all around the world.

Dietrich Fischer-Dieskau, born in 1925, is best known as a *lieder* singer, although he has become involved in the world of opera with considerable distinction. For many, his portrayal of the roles of Almaviva, Papageno and Falstaff are the definitive ones and, as one of the most distinguished musical scholars, he is revered for his encyclopaedic knowledge. He is married to the Romanian soprano Julia Varady.

Mirella Freni was born in Modena in 1935 (she had the same wet-nurse as Pavarotti) and showed signs of having a significant talent at the tender age of ten – by which time, it is said, she had already been singing excerpts from Verdi's *La traviata*. She is one of the greatest Italian sopranos to have emerged this century and her innate flair and love of the stage have equipped her to undertake all the great roles from the Romantic repertoire. In Jorge Lavelli's production of Gounod's *Faust* at the Paris Opera she was highly praised for her portrayal of Marguerite and has also achieved widespread acclaim in the roles of Susanna in *Le nozze di Figaro* and Zerlina in *Don Giovanni*.

Beniamino Gigli is another historic tenor whose recordings have survived and been transferred to CD. He had one of the most naturally beautiful voices that, thanks to his faultless technique and ease of vocal production, led him to sustain an enviably long career at the very top of the profession. Superlative in all the great lyric, romantic roles, his consummate artistry incorporating a versatility and quite extraordinary range are well worth hearing.

Tito Gobbi was born in 1913 and died at the age of seventy-one, in 1984, having left an indelible mark on the world of opera. One of the finest Italian baritones, his voice has not, in my opinion, been matched by any other baritone this century. Recordings are available of his work and one to be particularly recommended is his rendition of Scarpia from Puccini's *Tosca*.

Sometimes referred to as the male equal of Maria Callas, the two often played opposite each other in *Tosca*. There was a famous occasion at Covent Garden in 1964 when Callas leaned too far in to the flame of a candle and her wig caught alight. Gobbi hastily drew her into a fiery embrace, in the process of which he managed to beat out the sparks. A grateful Callas turned the mishap into a wonderfully dramatic impromptu episode, then whispered seductively in her saviour's ear '*Grazie*, Tito'. Gobbi recounts in his memoirs '*That* was Callas!'.

Barbara Hendricks is undoubtedly one of the most gifted of singers to have emerged in the last thirty years. Born in the USA in 1948, she has remarkable good looks and a beautiful voice to match. Her début was in *L'incoronazione di Poppea* by Monteverdi for San Francisco Opera in 1976 and since that time she has performed all over the world to great critical acclaim. Most recently she has taken the role of Ilia in a relatively new recording of Mozart's *Idomeneo*, while her performance in Richard Strauss's *Der Rosenkavalier* has been widely praised.

Marilyn Horne, born in the USA in 1929, has an extraordinary mezzo-soprano voice that also possesses great agility, thus making her eminently suitable for all the *bel canto* roles. Particularly noted for her Handel, Rossini and Bellini performances she has sometimes been said to be the 'mezzo equivalent of Joan Sutherland'.

Dmitri Hvorostovsky is one of the finest young talents to have emerged in recent years. Winner of the 'Singer of the World' competition held in Cardiff in 1989, he has gone on to make spectacular débuts at a number of the world's leading opera houses. His performance in Bellini's *I puritani* at the Royal Opera House, Covent Garden in May 1992, met with the highest praise.

Gwyneth Jones is one of Britain's best-loved sopranos. She has had a long and varied career in which she has always demonstrated an enormous power and a great enthusiasm for her work. Exceptional in roles like Brünnhilde from Wagner's *Ring*, she has also been widely praised for her performances in Verdi's *Aida* and Richard Strauss's *Elektra*.

Alfredo Kraus is a Spanish tenor of Austrian descent. He has a pure voice that is sometimes a little too focused in character for some people's taste but which is beautifully controlled nevertheless. He is also a very fine teacher and occasionally travels the world giving master classes to the most talented students emerging from the major musical academies.

Christa Ludwig is one of the very finest German mezzo-sopranos to appear in post-war years. Her voice is remarkably agile and has great projection – particularly in the high register – which is most unusual for a mezzo. This versatility has allowed her to move between mezzo and soprano roles, notably as Verdi's Lady Macbeth and Leonore in Beethoven's *Fidelio*. She is also very well suited to the big Wagner roles and has been praised too for her portrayal of Amneris in Verdi's *Aida*.

Sherrill Milnes is an American baritone who has been active on the operatic circuit for many years. He has a strong voice and an admirable degree of musical sensitivity which makes him constantly in demand for all the main Verdi and Mozart baritone roles.

Kurt Moll is the archetypal deep-bass singer from Germany, where he was born in 1938. He has an extremely wide repertoire and this, along with his good acting abilities, results in him being in demand all over the world. He is a very fine actor who has made excellent recordings of many of the Wagnerian roles, but he is also splendid in Strauss's *Der Rosenkavalier* and equally at home in the works of Mozart.

Birgit Nilsson is Sweden's finest export to the world of opera. One of the finest dramatic sopranos ever, she has a voice with a unique quality that has been brilliantly captured on record. Now in her seventies, she is helping the development of a number of up-and-coming young singers by giving master classes and holding summer schools in the UK and throughout Europe. In her prime Miss Nilsson was most praised for her dramatic roles in the works of Wagner and Richard Strauss, but her Turandot was apparently also a force to be reckoned with.

One of the great characters from the world of opera, Birgit Nilsson was involved in a crisp exchange with the late Herbert von Karajan when, during a rehearsal of *Tristan* in Vienna, her string of pearls snapped and cascaded all over the stage. As the cast scrabbled trying to retrieve them for the diva, Karajan asked: 'No doubt these are fabulously expensive pearls bought with your Metropolitan fees?' To which she promptly replied 'No, these are cheap imitation pearls bought with your Vienna fees!' A nice story that neatly illustrates the highly sensitive issue of money in opera.

Jessye Norman was brought up in Georgia in the southern USA. She has won numerous prizes and honours and her striking appearance and captivating stage presence have earned her the love and admiration of audiences the world over. After studying with the great French singer Pierre Bernac she embarked on her operatic career at the Berlin Opera, where her talents were immediately recognized. She was soon invited to perform at all the most distinguished opera houses in such diverse roles as the Countess in Mozart's *Le nozze di Figaro*, Madame Lidoine in Poulenc's *Dialogues des Carmélites* and Isolde in Wagner's *Tristan und Isolde*, to name but a few. One of the truly great singers of our time.

Peter Pears, the quintessential British tenor, had a very distinctive voice that helped make famous the operatic works of Benjamin Britten. He was an enormously talented and intelligent musician who, in partnership with Britten, created the roles of Albert Herring (in the opera of the same name), Vere in *Billy Budd* and many others.

Lucia Popp was born in Bratislava in 1939 and made her remarkable début at the 1963 Salzburg festival singing the virtuoso role of the Queen of Night in Mozart's *Die Zauberflöte*. She is a beautiful woman with a warm and engaging voice that has won the hearts of audiences everywhere. She made a lasting impression at the celebrated Vienna Opera, where she frequently appeared in her earlier years before moving on to Munich, Covent Garden and the Metropolitan in New York. Her recordings of the Mozart and Richard Strauss operas are all highly recommended.

Hermann Prey, who was born in Berlin in 1929, is one of the most distinguished German baritones. He has a very smooth, warm-sounding voice that is eminently suited to the works of Mozart. He is also recognized as a gifted interpreter of the Rossini roles.

Margaret Price is acknowledged as being one of the finest and most beautiful British lyric sopranos and her countless recordings include all the great repertoire by Mozart, Verdi, Wagner and Richard Strauss. She has a characteristically big voice that has an agility and intensity which enable her to take on both dramatic and coloratura roles with equal ease.

Leontyne Price, born in the USA in 1927, was the first black singer to gain international recognition. Her sensuous voice has a richness and vibrancy that has been enjoyed the world over and she has been widely recorded, particularly in the works of Verdi.

Ruggiero Raimondi is now regarded as the Italian bass of the moment. A regular performer at the Royal Opera House, Covent Garden, he is in demand at opera houses all around the world. His particular strengths are in the mainstream Mozart and Verdi roles and he appeared in the film of Mozart's *Marriage of Figaro* alongside Kiri Te Kanawa.

Samuel Ramey was born in 1940 in the USA. He possesses one of the most extraordinarily flexible bass voices to have emerged this century. The voice is not huge but has a beautiful quality that, coupled with his phenomenal technique, makes him to many opera companies the first choice for the florid bass roles of Handel, Rossini and Mozart.

Katia Ricciarelli has had a somewhat chequered career because, some say, her voice has never been totally secure. She has nevertheless made some absolutely stunning recordings and has attracted a large number of superlative reviews from critics the world over. Born in Italy in 1946, she's great as Mimì in Puccini's *La Bohème* and has been highly praised for her role as Desdemona in *Otello* by Verdi.

Elisabeth Schwarzkopf is regarded as one of the most distinguished performers of all time. She has a very highly developed sense of musicianship which she has brought to opera and *lieder* alike. Any recording featuring this great artist is worth exploring and particularly to be recommended are her recordings of Mozart and Richard Strauss. There's a lovely story that demonstrates Schwarzkopf's true professionalism. She was performing in *Der Rosenkavalier* when one of the dogs, claimed by the Animal-seller in the opera to be house-broken, did the unmentionable in her lap. The mess was appalling but Schwarzkopf calmly exited, borrowed a needle and thread and sewed a pocket to the front of the dress to hide the offending stain. Meanwhile, the tenor and flautist carried on valiantly and were soon rejoined by an unperturbed Schwarzkopf singing as beautifully as ever.

Renata Scotto, who was born in Italy in 1933, is another phenomenally talented diva. She has graced the world's finest opera stages in all the great lyric and coloratura roles and leaves a marvellous legacy of recordings for all to enjoy. Her performances of Violetta in Verdi's *La traviata* and her portrayal of Norma in Bellini's opera of the same name are particularly recommended.

Elisabeth Söderström is a Swedish soprano who is renowned for her wonderful pure voice and for her excellent grasp of several languages. Swedish is obviously not a natural language for opera but Söderström's unique gift is her supreme clarity of articulation and enunciation in all the main operatic languages. Her voice has a beauty and range of colours that in many roles is quite exquisite and her wide-ranging repertoire includes all the mainstream classical works and those by Janáček, Debussy and Richard Strauss.

Frederica von Stade was born in New Jersey in 1945. Possessing one of the most distinctive light and agile of mezzo-soprano voices, she is a true coloratura mezzo and, like Christa Ludwig, is also able to take on soprano roles with consummate ease, notably in Rossini's *La Cenerentola*.

Joan Sutherland is one of the all-time greats. She was born in Australia in 1926 and has won unanimous acclaim all around the world for her performances of the whole spectrum of operatic roles. Particularly fine in the *bel canto* roles by Handel, Donizetti (*Lucia di Lammermoor* is one of her very best) and Rossini, she can be equally at home in Wagner. She's an artist of considerable stature and, like Callas at her best, Pavarotti and many others, her strong physical presence seems fundamental to the vibrancy and glorious quality of her voice. She married the celebrated conductor of opera Richard Bonynge and together they made a lot of great music, recordings of which are plentiful.

Renata Tebaldi is recognized as one of the true Italian sopranos of the century. She didn't have the reputation of being the finest actress in the world, but as one can now hear her only on record that's not going to affect our judgement. She has made exquisite recordings of many of the great Italian masterpieces including all the big Puccini and Verdi operas.

Julia Varady made her début in 1962 as Fiordiligi (one of the sisters in Mozart's *Così fan tutte*) and moved to Frankfurt in 1970, where she has developed an international career largely from singing Mozart and Richard Strauss. Born in Romania in 1941, she has lent her talents also to performing a few twentieth-century eastern European operas, notably Bartók's *Bluebeard's Castle*. She is married to the distinguished baritone Dietrich Fischer-Dieskau.

Josephine Veasey, who was born in Britain in 1930, has made a number of very fine recordings as a mezzo-soprano in *Les troyens* (The Trojans) by Berlioz (as the character Dido) and in Wagner's *Tristan* as Brangäne. She has a very agile and technically secure voice that is extremely good in earlier works such as those by Handel, Rossini and Mozart.

Ingvar Wixell is a Swedish baritone of international repute who is a truly all-round musician. Before becoming one of the most celebrated baritones of this century he was an accomplished violinist and violist. He's performed at all of the world's leading opera houses and has that rare quality of being quite superb in everything he does.

THE DIRECTORS

When choosing operatic recordings the question of the director doesn't come into the proceedings, but when going to visit the opera it certainly has a bearing because the director is responsible for the way the opera is staged. We touched upon the issue of the ways in which directors can change the face of a traditional opera by fixing the piece in modern day dress or setting. Directors who bring this fresh approach to the works do so at some risk as such treatments are, of course, very subjective. Quite often the audience is so severely shocked at the outset of the performance that they find it hard to concentrate on what is going on: the treatment becomes more of a distraction than an integral part of the interpretation of the work. Although there have been a number of hugely successful innovative treatments in the staging of opera, it seems that the traditional approach still retains the most popular support amongst regular opera-goers.

The last fifty years have seen a number of outstanding directors who have had an extremely powerful effect on the way operas are staged. We will now take a brief look at these directors and their achievements.

Frederich Götz was the Artistic Director at the Deutsche Oper Berlin. He's a man of many talents and has gained the respect of all who work with him – singers and technical crews alike. His productions are always powerful and he's famous for a highly controversial staging of the *Ring* at London's Royal Opera House, Covent Garden.

Harry Küpfer is an even more controversial figure who is wildly creative in his approach. Love him or loathe him, he has made an enormous impact and has been highly influential in his time. He's best known for his work at the Deutsche Staatsoper, Berlin but he also attracted attention with his memorable production of Monteverdi's *Orfeo* – which he first brought to the UK and which he directed at Covent Garden – and the extraordinary staging of the *Ring* cycle at Bayreuth.

Jonathan Miller is one of Britain's best-known directors, at times highly controversial but always brilliantly creative in his thinking. He is responsible for the 'fascist' version of Puccini's *Tosca* in London. His exhilarating productions of *West Side Story* by the late Leonard Bernstein and Verdi's *Rigoletto* will be hard to beat in the coming years.

Jean-Pierre Ponnelle was a half-French, half-German genius who had an incredible track record of successes all around the world, particularly at La Scala, Vienna Opera and the Metropolitan in New York. A true master of the traditional opera, Ponnelle's talents were best suited to the mainstream repertoire of Mozart, Puccini and Verdi. He died under tragic circumstances, falling from the stage whilst directing a production-rehearsal of Bizet's *Carmen*, in Israel.

Luchino Visconti was one of the great talents from the world of operatic directors. He worked closely with Margherita Wallmann in staging the great triumphs of Maria Callas but his friendship and working relationship were cast aside by Callas when she got involved with Onassis. He was the master at staging the Italian operatic master- pieces by Bellini, Donizetti, Rossini and Puccini.

Franco Zeffirelli is the brilliant, innovative and dynamic Italian director who is equally at home working with the stage or screen – indeed, he even manages to bring a cinematic view and style to his treatments on the opera stage. Among his triumphs are the famous *Tosca* with Maria Callas at La Scala, Milan, and the first UK production of Donizetti's *Lucia di Lammermoor* which made Joan Sutherland a star at the Royal Opera House, Covent Garden, in 1953. Another production that was unanimously praised was *Turandot* at the Metropolitan Opera in New York, featuring Placido Domingo, while his films of Verdi's *La traviata* and *Otello* and Mascagni's *Cavalleria rusticana* are available for all to enjoy on video.

CHAPTER SEVEN

Where To Go To See An Opera

These days it's possible to see an opera in the most unlikely of places – sports arenas, in the open air, in stately homes and castles; almost every kind of building and setting has been used. Concert, reduced-cast and semi-staged performances are also becoming very popular as they are cost-effective to present and the audience experiences opera in intimate surroundings. While you lose the big spectacle, you gain a feeling of involvement through the proximity of the action. A number of companies have formed in recent years to satisfy this very market. Quite often the standard of performance is extremely high and, as well as reaching an enthusiastic and rapidly growing public, these productions provide a platform for young up-and-coming singers to gain experience of their craft.

However, it is at the major opera houses around the world that the high-profile performances take place. Here the very finest singers feature in productions staged by the most eminent directors. The sets are invariably lavish and impressive, while the lighting rigs are of a complexity and sophistication to match all but the most extravagant of pop concerts and stage shows.

The most famous opera companies and houses whose names appear in titles of recordings are the Royal Opera House Covent Garden (London), La Scala (Milan), The Metropolitan Opera (New York) and those based in Paris, Vienna and Berlin, not forgetting Bayreuth (Germany), the home of Wagner's operas, where the annual festival is held. Details of these, and of other famous opera companies around the world, and the opera houses at which they perform, are listed here.

UNITED KINGDOM

English National Opera
London Coliseum
St Martin's Lane
London WC2B 5LR
Tel: 071 836 2699

Glyndebourne Festival Opera & Touring Opera
Glyndebourne
Lewes
East Sussex BN8 5UU
Tel: 0273 812321

Opera North
Grand Theatre
46 New Briggate
Leeds
West Yorkshire LS1 6NU
Tel: 0532 445326

The Royal Opera
Royal Opera House
Covent Garden
London WC2E 9DD
Tel: 071 240 1200

Scottish Opera
Theatre Royal
Hope Street
Glasgow G2 3QA
Tel: 041 248 4567

Welsh National Opera
John Street
Cardiff
South Glamorgan CF1 4SP
Tel: 0222 464666

AUSTRALIA

Sydney Opera House Trust
Sydney Opera House
Bennelong Point
PO Box 4274
Sydney
NSW 2001
Tel: 2 250 7111

AUSTRIA

Wiener Staatsoper
Opernring 3
1010 Vienna
Tel: 5324 2655

CANADA

Canadian Opera Company
O'Keefe Center
Toronto
Ontario
Tel: 416 872 2262

L'Opéra de Montreal
Place des Arts
1501 rue Jeanne-Mance
Montreal H2X 1Z9
Tel: 514 521 5577

FRANCE

Opéra de Lyon
Place de la Comédie
69001 Lyon
Tel: 7 82 80 950

Opéra de La Bastille
120 Rue de Lyon
F-75012 Paris
Tel: 40 01 17 89

GERMANY

Deutsche Oper Berlin
34–37 Bismarck Strasse
1000 Berlin 1
Tel: 30 3438-1

Oper Frankfurt
Stadische Buhnen
Untermainanlage 11
Frankfurt
Tel: 69 25 62 529

Hamburgische Staatsoper
Postfach 302448
2000 Hamburg 36
Tel: 40 35680

Staatsoper München
Gartnerplatz Theater
8000 München 5
Tel: 89 20 24 1-1

Staatstheater Stuttgart
Oberer-Schlossgarten 6
7000 Stuttgart 1
Tel: 711 203 24 44

Bayreuth Festival
PO Box 2320
8580 Bayreuth
Tel: 921 20221

ITALY

Teatro Alla Scala
Via Filodramatica 2
Milan
Tel: 2 809 129

Teatro Comunale di Firenze
Via Solferino 15
I-50123 Florence
Tel: 55 27791

Teatro dell'Opera
Piazza B. Gigli 8
I-00184
Rome
Tel: 46 36 41

Teatro La Fenice Venezia
Campo S. Fantin 2519
I-30124
Venice
Tel: 786 511

THE NETHERLANDS

Netherlands Opera
De Nederlandse Opera
Waterlooplein 22
1011 PG Amsterdam
Tel: 20 255454

SCANDINAVIA

Den Norske Opera
Stortgaten 23
0184 Oslo 1
Norway
Tel: 2 42 94 75

Finnish National Opera
Bulevardi 23-27
PL 188
00181 Helsinki
Finland
Tel: 90 12921

Royal Danish Opera
The Royal Theatre
PO Box 2185
1017 Copenhagen K
Denmark
Tel: 1 32 20 20

Royal Swedish Opera
Kungliga Teatern
8 10322 Stockholm
Sweden
Tel: 8 791 4300

United States of America

Houston Grand Opera
Jones Hall
615 Louisiana
Houston
Texas 77002
Tel: 713 546 0240

Metropolitan Opera
Metropolitan Opera House
Lincoln Center
New York
NY 10023
Tel: 212 799 3100

San Francisco Opera
War Memorial Opera House
301 Van Ness Avenue
San Francisco
CA 94102
Tel: 415 861 4008

Bibliography

There are scores of books about opera for the avid reader to pursue. Many are written in a rather formal style and in the main are aimed at the already well-informed opera lover, assuming quite a high degree of reader knowledge and experience. In this category excellent texts are to be found in the *Concise Dictionary of Opera* (Oxford University Press, London, 1978) by Harold Rosenthal and John Warrack. Arthur Jacobs and Stanley Sadie have also produced a fine guide in *The Pan Book of Opera* (Pan Books, London, 1964 and 1984). Both books come highly recommended.

Kobbé's *Complete Opera Book* (Bodley Head, London, 1976) is the definitive guide for those seeking synopses of all the popular operas and I have often found the *English National Opera Guides* (ENO/John Caulder, London) to be of great value. They give translations of the texts, as well as useful background information and essays on each work and are eminently user-friendly.

Other instructive books worthy of special mention are:

John Lazarus: *The Opera Handbook* (Longman, 1987)
Ernest Newman: *Wagner Nights* (Bodley Head, 1949)
Stanley Sadie: *Mozart* (The New Grove, 1982)
Various: *Masters of Italian Opera* (The New Grove, 1983)

For a look at the lighter side of opera, turn to:

Ethan Mordden: *Opera Anecdotes* (Oxford University Press, 1985)
Hugh Vickers: *Great Operatic Disasters* (Papermac, 1979)

Index

Operas and arias are indexed under both English and foreign names where appropriate. **Bold titles** refer to the 'Top Ten' operas, arias and composers on the cassette. **Bold page numbers** show main references for subjects with several entries.

OPERA

We have compiled a special collection of the major pieces of music referred to in the book. *Get Into Opera Volume 1* is available on CD or cassette and consists of over an hour of the finest performances from around the world.

To obtain the CD or cassette by post, simply complete this order form and send a cheque or postal order, made payable to *Music Men Productions Ltd.*, to the address given below. Please allow 28 days for delivery. (Overseas customers are asked to send the sterling equivalent and to add £1.50.)

Get Into Opera cassette £5.99 each   £ ....

Get Into Opera CD £9.99 each   £ ....

Also available by post

Get Into Classical Music cassette £5.09 each   £ ....

Get Into Classical Music CD £8.99 each   £ ....

(prices include postage and packing) TOTAL: £.................

Our address is:
Music Men Productions Ltd
PO Box 2807
London W6 0JW

Please print your name and address clearly and attach this order form to your payment:

Name: ....

Address: ....

....

................................Postcode...........